THiNK

STUDENT'S BOOK 1 **A2**

Herbert Puchta, Jeff Stranks & Peter Lewis-Jones

CAMBRIDGE
UNIVERSITY PRESS

CONTENTS

	FUNCTIONS & SPEAKING	GRAMMAR	VOCABULARY
Unit 1 Having fun p 12	Talking about routines and everyday activities Expressing likes and dislikes Giving warnings and stating prohibition	Present simple review *like + -ing* Adverbs of frequency	Hobbies **WordWise:** Collocations with *have*
Unit 2 Money and how to spend it p 20	Role play: Buying things in a shop Talking about what people are doing at the moment	Present continuous Verbs of perception Present simple vs. present continuous	Shops Clothes
Review Units 1 & 2 pages 28–29			
Unit 3 Food for life p 30	Talking about food Ordering a meal Apologising	Countable and uncountable nouns *a/an, some, any* *How much / many, a lot of / lots of* *too* and *(not) enough*	Food and drink Adjectives to talk about food **WordWise:** Expressions with *have got*
Unit 4 Family ties p 38	Talking about families Asking for permission	Possessive adjectives and pronouns *whose* and possessive *'s* *was / were*	Family members Feelings
Review Units 3 & 4 pages 46–47			
Unit 5 It feels like home p 48	Talking about events in the past Making suggestions Role play: Buying furniture for your youth club	Past simple (regular verbs) Modifiers: *quite, very, really*	Parts of a house and furniture Adjectives with *-ed / -ing* **WordWise:** Phrasal verbs with *look*
Unit 6 Best friends p 56	Saying what you like doing alone and with others Talking about past events Talking about friends and friendships	Past simple (irregular verbs) Double genitive Past simple questions	Past time expressions Personality adjectives
Review Units 5 & 6 pages 64–65			
Unit 7 The easy life p 66	Giving advice Talking about rules Asking for repetition and clarification Role play: A phone call	*have to / don't have to* *should / shouldn't* *mustn't* vs. *don't have to*	Gadgets Housework **WordWise:** Expressions with *like*
Unit 8 Sporting moments p 74	Talking about sports Talking about feelings	Past continuous Past continuous vs. past simple *when* and *while*	Sport and sports verbs Adverbs of sequence
Review Units 7 & 8 pages 82–83			
Unit 9 The wonders of the world p 84	Talking about the weather Paying compliments	Comparative adjectives Superlative adjectives *can / can't* for ability	Geographical features The weather **WordWise:** Phrases with *with*
Unit 10 Around town p 92	Talking about plans Inviting and making arrangements Discussing ideas for an imaginary film	*be going to* for intentions Present continuous for arrangements Adverbs	Places in a town Things in town: compound nouns
Review Units 9 & 10 pages 100–101			
Unit 11 Future bodies p 102	Role play: A health problem Making predictions Sympathising	*will / won't* for future predictions First conditional Time clauses with *when / as soon as*	Parts of the body *when* and *if* **WordWise:** Expressions with *do*
Unit 12 Travellers' tales p 110	Talking about travel and transport Talking about life experiences Role play: Life as a bus driver / flight attendant	Present perfect simple Present perfect with *ever / never* Present perfect vs. past simple	Transport and travel Travel verbs

PRONUNCIATION	THINK	SKILLS	
/s/, /z/, /ɪz/ sounds	**Values:** Taking care of yourself **Self esteem:** Why it's good to have a hobby	Reading	Quiz: Do you take good care of yourself? Blog: So what do you do in your free time? Photostory: Olivia's new hobby
		Writing	Writing about routines
		Listening	Conversations about hobbies
Contractions	**Values:** Fashion and clothes **Train to Think:** Exploring numbers	Reading	Soap opera: Shopping Webchat: How not to spend money Culture: World markets
		Writing	An informal email to say what you're doing
		Listening	Shop dialogues
Vowel sounds: /ɪ/ and /iː/	**Values:** Food and health **Self esteem:** Being happy	Reading	Article: Food facts or food fiction? Blog: My brother's cooking Photostory: The picnic
		Writing	A paragraph about your favourite or least favourite meal
		Listening	Ordering food in a café
-er /ə/ at the end of words	**Values:** TV families **Train to Think:** Making inferences	Reading	Article: TV Families Article: The swimming pool heroes Culture: Around the world on Children's Day
		Writing	An invitation
		Listening	Why my family drive me mad
-ed endings /d/, /t/, /ɪd/	**Values:** Community spirit **Self esteem:** Feeling safe	Reading	Article: The Lego House Blog: Dad gets it right! (finally) Photostory: Hey, look at that guy!
		Writing	A blog post and a summary of a text
		Listening	What is home?
Stressed syllables in words	**Values:** Friendship and loyalty **Train to Think:** Making decisions	Reading	Article: Together Article: How we met Culture: Friendship myths
		Writing	An apology
		Listening	A story about Cristiano Ronaldo
Vowel sounds: /ʊ/ and /uː/	**Values:** Caring for people and the environment **Self esteem:** Classroom rules	Reading	Article: Just because I didn't want to take a bath Website: Product reviews Photostory: The treasure hunt
		Writing	A paragraph about housework
		Listening	Radio programme – advice for young inventors
Strong and weak forms of *was* and *were*	**Values:** Trying, winning and losing **Train to Think:** Sequencing	Reading	Article: If you don't give up, you can't fail Web forum: Your favourite sports fails! Culture: The Olympic Games – the good and the not-so-good
		Writing	An article about a sporting event
		Listening	Teens talking about sport
Vowel sounds: /ɪ/ and /aɪ/	**Values:** Valuing our world **Self esteem:** Being brave is …	Reading	Article: An amazing place Article: Could you live there? Photostory: The competition
		Writing	An email about a place in the article
		Listening	Interview with a Kalahari bushman
Voiced /ð/ and unvoiced /θ/ consonants	**Values:** Appreciating other cultures **Train to Think:** Problem solving	Reading	Blogs: Alice's world, The life of Brian Letters to a newspaper: Our town: what's wrong and what can we do about it? Culture: Ghost towns around the world
		Writing	An informal email
		Listening	A conversation between people arranging to go out
The /h/ consonant sound	**Values:** Exercise and health **Self esteem:** Getting help	Reading	Article: Changing bodies Webchats: Crazy things that parents say to their kids Photostory: The phone call
		Writing	A phone message
		Listening	Dialogues about physical problems
Sentence stress	**Values:** Travel broadens the mind **Train to Think:** Exploring differences	Reading	Blog: The non-stop traveller Interview: The taxi driver Culture: Hard journeys for schoolchildren
		Writing	An essay about someone you admire
		Listening	A traveller talking to children at his old school

WELCOME

A ALL ABOUT ME
Personal information

1 🔊 **1.02** **Put the dialogue in order. Number the boxes. Listen and check.**

1	ALEX	Hi. I'm Alex.
	ALEX	I'm fourteen. How about you?
	ALEX	The United States.
	ALEX	Hello, Fabiola. Where are you from?
	ABIOLA	Me? I'm fourteen, too.
	FABIOLA	I'm from Italy. And you?
	FABIOLA	Hi, Alex. My name's Fabiola.
	FABIOLA	Cool! How old are you, Alex?

2 🔊 **1.03** **Complete the dialogue with the phrases in the list. Listen and check.**

are | meet | this | too

ALEX   Fabiola – ¹_____ is my friend Ravi.

RAVI   Hi, Fabiola. Nice to ²_____ you.

FABIOLA   Nice to meet you, ³_____ , Ravi.
          And this is my friend: her name's Patrizia.

PATRIZIA Hi, guys. How ⁴_____ you? I'm Patrizia.
          Patrizia Lambertucci.

3 **SPEAKING** **Imagine you are a famous person. Work in pairs, then groups.**

1 Tell your partner who you are.

2 Introduce your partner to others in the group.

> Hi, I'm Ryan Gosling.

> Hello, my name's Rihanna. And this is my friend, Barack Obama.

Nationalities and *be*

4 **Complete the names of the countries (add the consonants).**

1 _ _ a _ i _

2 _ _ e a _
_ _ i _ a i _

3 the _ e _ _ er-
a _ _ _ _

4 _ o _ o _ _ i a

5 I _ _ a _ _

6 _ e _ i _ o

7 _ u _ _ i a

8 _ _ _ a i _

9 _ u _ _ e _

10 the U _ i _ e _
_ _ a _ e _

11 A _ _ e _ _ i _ a

12 _ _ e _ _ _ i u _

Carlos
0 *He's Brazilian.*

Sandra
1 *She's* _____

Liam and Jane
2 _____

Natasha and Anna
3 _____

Ricardo
4 _____

Burcu
5 _____

Lotte
6 _____

Giovanni
7 _____

Andrea
8 _____

Raul and Luis
9 _____

5 What nationality are the people? Write the sentences.

6 ◀) 1.04 Complete the dialogue using the correct forms of the verb *to be*. Then listen and check.

FABIOLA So, Ravi – where 0 __*are*__ you from?

RAVI Me? I 1 _____ from Britain. Alex here 2 _____ from the United States, but I 3 _____ British.

PATRIZIA But, 4 _____ your name British?

RAVI Oh, good question. Well, no it 5 _____ . My parents 6 _____ from India and so my name 7 _____ from India too. But my sister Anita and I were both born here, so we 8 _____ 100% British.

FABIOLA That 9 _____ cool. I think your name 10 _____ really nice.

RAVI Thank you! And you two, 11 _____ you both Italian?

PATRIZIA That 12 _____ right. But we 13 _____ not from the same city. I 14 _____ from Milan and Fabiola 15 _____ from Bari. We 16 _____ students at the language school here.

Names and addresses

7 ◀) 1.05 Ravi phones for a taxi. Listen and complete the information.

▰▱▰ COOPER'S TAXIS ▰▱▰

Booking form

Taxi for	1 _____
Going to	2 _____
Pick up at	3 _____ am/pm
From	4 _____ Street
Number of passengers	5 _____

8 ◀) 1.06 Now listen to a phone call. Correct each of these sentences.

0 Alex phones Patrizia.
   No — Patrizia phones Alex.
1 They met last Wednesday.
2 There's a party at Patrizia's place next Friday.
3 The party starts at seven thirty.
4 Patrizia lives at 134 Markam Avenue.
5 Her phone number is 0788 224 234.

B WHAT'S THAT?

Things in the classroom

1 Look at the pictures. Write the correct number next to each word.

board ☐   book ☐   CD ☐   chair ☐   desk ☐   floor ☐

pen ☐   pencil ☐   ruler ☐   window ☐   door ☐   notebook ☐

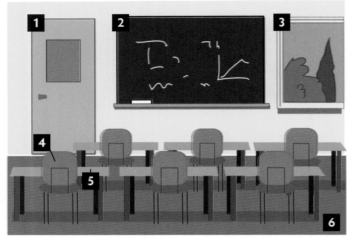

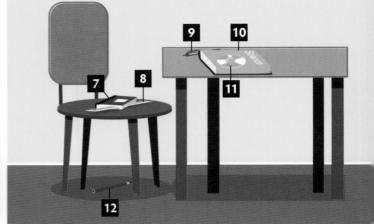

Prepositions of place

2 Look at the pictures. Complete each sentence with a preposition from the list (you will use some words more than once).

on | between | in | under | in front of | behind

0 The notebook is ___*on*___ the chair.

1 The pencil is _____ the floor.

2 The pencil is _____ the chair.

3 The book is _____ the desk.

4 The pen is _____ the book.

5 The ruler is _____ the notebook.

6 The board is _____ the door and the window.

7 The book is _____ the pen.

Classroom language

3 ◀)) 1.07 Complete each sentence with a word from the list. Listen and check.

ask | again | mean | hand | don't
page | me | say | spell | understand

1 Excuse _____ .

2 Can I _____ a question, please?

3 Can you say that _____ , please?

4 How do you _____ *cansado* in English?

5 Open your books at _____ 21.

6 Put your _____ up if you know the answer.

7 Sorry, I _____ know.

8 Sorry, I don't _____ .

9 What does this word _____ ?

10 Excuse me. How do you _____ that word?
Is it T-I-R-E-D or T-Y-R-E-D?

4 ◀)) 1.08 Use one of the sentences in Exercise 3 to complete each mini-dialogue. Listen and check.

1 TEACHER Good morning, everyone.
   STUDENTS Good morning.
   TEACHER OK. Let's start. _____

2 TEACHER So, Michael, what's the answer?
   MICHAEL _____
   TEACHER That's OK. What about you, Susie?

3 STUDENT _____ ,
   Mrs McFarlane. I've got a question.
   TEACHER Yes, what is it?
   STUDENT _____ : 'fascinating'?
   TEACHER It means: 'very, very interesting'.

5 ◀)) 1.09 Put the lines in order to make a dialogue. Listen and check.

☐ A E-N-O-U-G-H.

☐ A No, that's completely wrong!

1 A How do you think you spell the word 'enough'?

☐ A No, that's really how you spell it.

☐ B OK, how do you spell it, then?

☐ B Oh. Let me think. Is it E-N-U-F-F?

☐ B You're kidding!

6 SPEAKING Work in pairs. Think of a word in English. Can your partner spell it?

How do you spell 'awful'?   A-W-F-U-L.

That's right.

Object pronouns

7 Complete each sentence with the correct pronoun.

0 She's a good teacher – we like _*her*_ a lot.

1 My pens are under your desk. Can you get _____ , please?

2 I've got a new book – I'm going to read _____ this afternoon.

3 Sorry, can you speak more loudly? I can't hear _____ .

4 I really can't do this homework – can you help _____?

5 He doesn't understand so please help _____ .

6 We like our teacher. She gives _____ good marks!

this / that / these / those

8 Match the pictures and sentences.

1 What does this word mean?

2 What does that word mean?

3 These books are heavy.

4 Those books are heavy.

9 Complete the email by writing one word in each space.

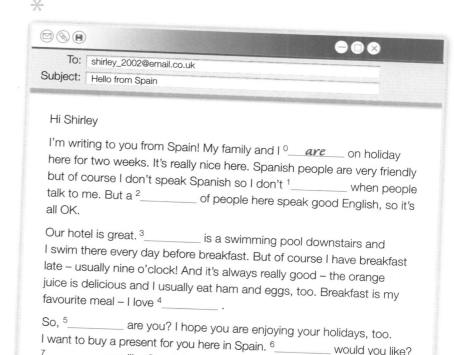

To: shirley_2002@email.co.uk

Subject: Hello from Spain

Hi Shirley

I'm writing to you from Spain! My family and I ⁰ _*are*_ on holiday here for two weeks. It's really nice here. Spanish people are very friendly but of course I don't speak Spanish so I don't ¹_____ when people talk to me. But a ²_____ of people here speak good English, so it's all OK.

Our hotel is great. ³_____ is a swimming pool downstairs and I swim there every day before breakfast. But of course I have breakfast late – usually nine o'clock! And it's always really good – the orange juice is delicious and I usually eat ham and eggs, too. Breakfast is my favourite meal – I love ⁴_____ .

So, ⁵_____ are you? I hope you are enjoying your holidays, too. I want to buy a present for you here in Spain. ⁶_____ would you like? ⁷_____ you like Spanish music? Write and tell ⁸_____ , OK?

Have a good time and write soon.

Love

Howard

C ABOUT TIME
Days and dates

1 🔊 **1.10** Listen and (circle) the correct information.

OLIVER	Hi, Shona. Why are you so happy today?
SHONA	Because it's the ¹*21st / 22nd / 23rd* February.
OLIVER	And what's special about that date?
SHONA	It's my birthday!
OLIVER	Really! Happy birthday, Shona.
SHONA	Thanks. I'm ²*12 / 13 / 14* today.
OLIVER	Lucky you!
SHONA	When is your birthday, Oliver?
OLIVER	It's in ³*August / September / October*.
SHONA	What date?
OLIVER	The ⁴*11th / 12th / 13th*. I think it's on a ⁵*Tuesday / Thursday / Friday* this year.

2 🔊 **1.11** Complete the names of the days and months. Listen and check.

DAYS

1 M o n d a y   5 F _ _ _ _ _ _
2 T _ _ sd _ _   6 S _ _ _ _ r _ _ y
3 W _ _ n _ _ d _ _   7 S _ _ _ _ _ _
4 _ h u _ _ _ _ _ y

MONTHS

1 J _ _ u _ _ y   7 J _ _ y
2 F _ bru _ _ _   8 A _ _ u _ _
3 M _ _ _ _ h   9 S _ _ _ _ mber
4 _ p _ _ l   10 O _ _ _ _ _ er
5 M _ _   11 _ _ vem _ _ _
6 J _ _ _ _   12 D _ _ _ _ _ _ _

3 Draw lines to match the numbers and the words.

first	22nd
second	3rd
third	12th
fourth	4th
fifth	15th
twelfth	2nd
fifteenth	5th
twentieth	31st
twenty-second	1st
thirty-first	20th

4 🔊 **1.12** How do you say these numbers? Listen and check.

7th | 11th | 14th | 19th | 23rd | 28th | 30th

5 🔊 **1.13** Listen and write the people's birthdays.

1 _4th August_   2 _____

3 _____   4 _____

5 _____   6 _____

6 **SPEAKING** Walk around the classroom. Ask and answer questions. Whose birthday is close to your birthday?

When's your birthday?   *It's on 17th March.*

My day

7 Put the pictures in the order you do them.

A ☐
I go to school.

B ☐
I get home.

C ☐
I go to bed.

D ☐
I have dinner.

E ☐
I have breakfast.

F ☐
I get up.

G ☐
I do my homework.

H ☐
I have lunch.

8 Look at the sentences in Exercise 7. Write them in the correct column <u>for you</u>.

Morning	Afternoon	Evening
I get up.		

9 Match the clocks and the times.

1 It's half past eight.
2 It's quarter past three.
3 It's eleven o'clock.
4 It's six o'clock.
5 It's eight o'clock.
6 It's quarter to eight.
7 It's ten to one.
8 It's twenty past ten.

A 2

I _get home._

B ☐

I _____

C ☐

I _____

D ☐

I _____

E ☐

I _____

F ☐

I _____

G ☐

I _____

H ☐

I _____

> **LOOK!**
> midday to midnight = pm
> midnight to midday = am
> 12 am = midnight
> 12 pm = midday
>
> 1 am = 1 o'clock in the early morning
> 1 pm = 1 o'clock in the afternoon

10 🔊 1.14 Listen to Leah. Write about her day under the pictures in Exercise 9.

11 SPEAKING Work in pairs. Talk about your day.

> I get up at half past seven.

> I have lunch at twelve o'clock.

9

D MY THINGS
My possessions

1 Read Chloës's blog and tick (✓) the photos of the things she has got.

2 Work in pairs. How many things about Chloë can you write in each list?

PERSONAL POSSESSIONS: *TV*_____ , *laptop*_____ ,
_____ , _____ , _____ , _____

PETS: *cat*_____ , _____ , _____ ,

have got

3 Complete the table with *have, has, haven't* or *hasn't*.

Positive	Negative
I've (have) got a dog.	I haven't (have not) got a cat.
You ¹_____ (have) got a dog.	You ⁵_____ (have not) got a cat.
He's (has) got a dog.	He hasn't (has not) got a cat.
She ²_____ (has) got a dog.	She ⁶_____ (has not) got a cat.
We ³_____ (have) got a dog.	We ⁷_____ (have not) got a cat.
They ⁴_____ (have) got a dog.	They ⁸_____ (have not) got a cat.

Questions	Short answers
Have I got a pet?	Yes, you have. / No, you haven't.
⁹_____ you got a pet?	Yes, I ¹³_____ / No, I ¹⁴_____
Has he got a pet?	Yes, he has / No, he hasn't.
¹⁰_____ she got a pet?	Yes, she ¹⁵_____ / No, she ¹⁶_____
¹¹_____ we got a pet?	Yes, we ¹⁷_____ / No, we ¹⁸_____
¹²_____ they got a pet?	Yes, they ¹⁹_____ / No, they ²⁰_____

4 Complete the sentences with *have, has, haven't* or *hasn't* so they are true for you.

1 I _____ got a tablet.
2 My dad _____ got a computer.
3 I _____ got a dog.
4 My best friend _____ got a brother.
5 I _____ got a TV in my bedroom.
6 My mum _____ got a car.

5 **SPEAKING** Walk around the classroom. Find someone who has got ...

1 a red bike
2 a cat and a dog
3 an English dictionary
4 an email address
5 two brothers or sisters
6 a smart phone
7 an unusual pet
8 a house with a garden

Have you got a bike?   *Yes, I have.*

What colour is it?

WELCOME!

Hi, my name's Chloë,

I've got a bike – it's really my favourite thing!

I haven't got a pet but I'd love a cat or maybe something unusual like a lizard.

I haven't got a smart phone. I want one for my next birthday.

I've got an MP3 player and I've got a tablet. I haven't got a laptop. My dad's got one and I sometimes use that.

I've got a TV in my bedroom. And I've got a camera, a small one but it's nice.

I'm a very lucky girl.

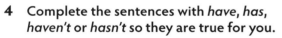

I like and *I'd like*

6 Match the pictures and the sentences.

A ☐

B ☐

C ☐

D ☐

1 I like apples!	3 I'd like six apples.
2 I'd like a hot shower!	4 I like hot showers.

7 🔊 **1.15 Complete with *I like* or *I'd like*. Listen and check.**

0 A What's your favourite food?
  B _*I like*_ curry best.

1 A Can I help you?
  B Yes, _____ a kilo of oranges.

2 A _____ an ice cream, please.
  B Chocolate or strawberry?

3 A What do you want to watch?
  B Well, _____ films, so can we watch a film, please?

4 A _____ cycling. Do you?
  B Not much. I think running's better.

5 A Do you want pizza or lasagne?
  B Well, pizza's my favourite food – but today, _____ lasagne, please!

8 Complete with the words in the list.

banana | orange juice | tuna | biscuit

Picnic Box
Sandwiches:
cheese or ¹_____

Desserts:
cake or ²_____

Fruit:
apple or ³_____

Drinks:
water or ⁴_____

9 🔊 **1.16 Listen to the dialogue. What does Max choose for his lunch? Circle the food above.**

10 🔊 **1.16 Write the questions in the spaces to complete part of the dialogue. Listen again and check.**

What fruit would you like?
Have you got bananas?
What would you like for lunch today?
Would you like a tuna sandwich or a cheese sandwich?

DINNER LADY	Hi, Max. ¹_____
MAX	I'd like a picnic box, please.
DINNER LADY	²_____
MAX	A cheese sandwich, please.
DINNER LADY	³_____
MAX	⁴_____
DINNER LADY	Yes, we have.
MAX	A banana, please.

11 **SPEAKING** **Work in pairs. Make a picnic box for your partner. Ask and answer questions.**

What would you like for ... ?

Would you like a ... or ... ?

11

1 | HAVING FUN

OBJECTIVES

FUNCTIONS: talking about routines and everyday activities; expressing likes and dislikes; giving warnings and stating prohibition

GRAMMAR: present simple review; *like + -ing*; adverbs of frequency

VOCABULARY: hobbies; collocations with *have*

A

B

C

E

F

G

D

H

READING

1 Match the activities in the list with the photos. Write 1–8 in the boxes.

1 sleeping	5 reading
2 doing homework	6 dancing
3 playing football	7 tidying up
4 studying	8 singing

2 Are these activities fun? Write *always*, *sometimes* or *never*.

1 Sleeping is _____ fun.
2 Doing homework is _____ fun.
3 Playing football is _____ fun.
4 Studying is _____ fun.
5 Reading is _____ fun.
6 Dancing is _____ fun.
7 Tidying up is _____ fun.
8 Singing is _____ fun.

3 **SPEAKING** Work in groups of three and compare your ideas from Exercise 2.

> I think dancing is always fun.

> I think it's sometimes fun.

4 **SPEAKING** Think of more activities and say what you think.

> Riding a bike is always fun.

> Doing housework is never fun.

5 1.17 Read and listen to the quiz. Match the pictures with the questions in the quiz. Write 1–7 in the boxes.

Do you take good care of yourself?

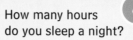
D

Does your teacher give you a lot of homework? Do your parents always want your bedroom tidy? School work, housework; life's not always easy. There are a lot of things to do and there isn't always time to do it all. But in your busy life it's important to think about yourself. It's important to do things you like, things that make you happy. Everyone needs fun.

So take our quiz and find out. Do you take good care of yourself?

4 How many hours do you sleep a night?
a) nine to ten hours
b) about eight
c) less than eight

5 Do you like exercise?
a) Yes, exercise is fun.
b) It's OK.
c) No. It's really boring.

1 Do you smile a lot?
a) Yes, I smile all the time.
b) I only smile when I'm happy.
c) My best friend says I don't smile very often.

A

6 Do you like puzzles and crosswords?
a) I love them.
b) They're OK.
c) I don't really like them. They're boring.

E

B

2 How many hobbies do you have?
a) I've got lots of hobbies.
b) One or two.
c) I don't have any hobbies.

F

G

3 When do you relax?
a) In the morning, afternoon and in the evening.
b) I relax when I have time.
c) I never relax. I'm always busy.

C

7 Which of these things do you do most?
a) Talk with friends and family.
b) Meet friends online.
c) Watch TV and play computer games.

■ THiNK VALUES ■

Taking care of yourself

1 Which questions in the quiz tell us that these things are important for us?

a `7` Being with people
b ☐ Enjoying exercise
c ☐ Sleep
d ☐ Getting rest
e ☐ Giving your brain exercise
f ☐ Being positive
g ☐ Having interests

YOUR SCORE:

Mostly As: You take good care of yourself. You know how to have fun and enjoy life.

Mostly Bs: You take care of yourself OK, but can you do more? Try and find more time for yourself.

Mostly Cs: You don't take good care of yourself. Try and have more fun.

2 **SPEAKING** Compare your ideas with a partner.

Question 7 shows us that being with people is important.

GRAMMAR
Present simple review

1 Complete the sentences with the words in the list. Check your answers in the quiz on page 13.

~~relax~~ | do | does | don't | says

0 I never ___relax___ .
1 My best friend _____ I don't smile very often.
2 I _____ really like them.
3 _____ your teacher give you a lot of homework?
4 _____ you like exercise?

2 Look at the sentences in Exercise 1 and the table. Complete the rule with *do*, *does*, *don't* or *doesn't*.

Positive	Negative
I **like** milk.	I **don't like** milk.
You **like** milk.	You **don't like** milk.
He/She/It **likes** milk.	He/She/It **doesn't like** milk.
We **like** milk.	We **don't like** milk.
They **like** milk.	They **don't like** milk.

Questions	Short answers	
Do I **like** milk?	Yes, you **do**.	No, you **don't**.
Do you **like** milk?	Yes, I **do**.	No, I **don't**.
Does he/she/it **like** milk?	Yes, he/she/it **does**.	No, he/she/it **doesn't**.
Do we **like** milk?	Yes, we **do**.	No, we **don't**.
Do they **like** milk?	Yes, they **do**.	No, they **don't**.

RULE: Use the present simple for things that happen regularly or that are always true.

In positive sentences:
- with *I, you, we* and *they*, use the base form of the verb.
- with *he, she* and *it*, add *-s* (or *-es* with verbs that end *-s, -sh, -ch, -x,* or *-z*).

In negative sentences:
- with *I, you, we* and *they*, use [1]_____ .
- with *he, she* and *it*, use [2]_____ .

In questions:
- with *I, you, we* and *they*, use the auxiliary [3]_____ .
- with *he, she* and *it*, use the auxiliary [4]_____ .

3 Complete the sentences. Use the present simple of the verbs.

0 I ___don't like___ (not like) roller coasters. I ___get___ (get) really scared on them.
1 My dad _____ (not sleep) a lot. He only _____ (need) five or six hours.
2 A _____ you _____ (study) English?
  B Yes, I _____ .
3 My dad _____ (cook) really well but he says he _____ (not enjoy) it.
4 A _____ your sister _____ (play) in the school football team?
  B No, she _____ .
5 My grandparents _____ (not like) travelling. They _____ (prefer) to stay at home.
6 My brother _____ (watch) TV all day. He _____ (not do) anything else.

> Workbook page 10

Pronunciation
/s/, /z/, /ɪz/ sounds
Go to page 120.

VOCABULARY
Hobbies

1 Complete the phrases with the words in the list.

~~play~~ | write | keep | take | be | collect

0 to ___play___ an instrument
1 to _____ in a club
2 to _____ a blog
3 to _____ photos
4 to _____ a pet
5 to _____ things

2 **SPEAKING** Work in pairs. Ask questions about the hobbies in the pictures.

Do you play an instrument?   *What do you play?*

Do you collect something? What ...?

> Workbook page 12

YOUTH CLUB

NAME: **Peter Summers**
ADDRESS: 51 Willow Avenue
PHONE: 07734 384 587
MEMBERSHIP NUMBER: 09173

LISTENING

1 🔊 **1.20** **Listen to the conversations. Match each one with a picture.**

A ☐

STOP
B ☐

C ☐

2 🔊 **1.20** **Listen again. Complete the sentences with the names in the list.**

~~Tom~~ | Carla | Lisa | Lisa's dad | James | James's mum

0 _____Tom_____ has got a headache.

1 _____ wants to join a football club.

2 _____ doesn't have time to relax.

3 _____ thinks music is good for relaxing.

4 _____ wants to be a famous piano player.

5 _____ thinks football is for boys.

■ THiNK SELF-ESTEEM ■

Why it's good to have a hobby

1 Circle **the person from Listening Exercise 1.**

I think it's good to have a hobby because …

1 you can make new friends.
A Carla   **B** Lisa   **C** James

2 it helps you relax.
A Carla   **B** Lisa   **C** James

3 you can discover you have new talents.
A Carla   **B** Lisa   **C** James

2 **Copy the diagram into your notebooks and complete it with the hobbies in the list.**

playing the piano | joining a tennis club
collecting stamps | writing a blog
dancing | cooking | watching TV
playing online games | taking photos

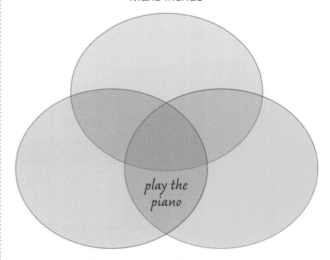

Make friends

play the piano

Relax   *Discover your talents*

3 SPEAKING **Work in pairs. Compare diagrams with your partner.**

> *Playing the piano is good. It helps you to relax.*

4 **What hobbies have you got? Think about why they are good for you. Make notes.**

5 **Tell your partner about your hobbies.**

> *I dance. I'm not very good but it helps me to relax.*

READING

1 Read the blog and answer the questions.

1 How many people like collecting things?
2 Who has got the strangest hobby?

So what do you do in your free time?

OK, we know you all like watching TV and playing computer games but we want to know some of the other things you do when you've got some free time. Write us a line or two and let us know.

Posted on January 22

NATHAN
I love collecting autographs of my friends and family. Now I want to get some from some famous people.

CHLOE
I enjoy lying on my back and looking at the clouds. I try to find different shapes in them. It's really relaxing and I occasionally fall asleep doing it.

IZZY
Once a week my granddad takes me out for a milkshake. I love listening to his stories. It's the best.

ADAM
I can't stand walking to school so I sometimes invent little games to help pass the time. For example I try to think of an animal, or football team or city for every letter of the alphabet.

LIZ
I like doing my homework as soon as I get home from school. Is there something wrong with me?

REBECCA
I really like going for a walk on my own in the forest near our house. There's always something interesting to see and I never get bored.

LEWIS
I collect bottle tops. I always take one home every time I go to a restaurant.

DYLAN
I like watching the news on TV. I watch it every day. My friends think I'm weird.

KUBA
I hate being on my own. So when I am by myself I usually start talking to my imaginary friends. But don't tell anyone!

JASMINE
I rarely get bored but if I do I just go to the library and get a book to learn about something new. It works every time.

DAISY
I like writing poems. I often write a poem when I've got nothing to do.

2 Read the sentences. Which of the people above do you think is saying each one?

0 *A country that starts with R? Easy: Russia.* — *Adam*

1 *Have you got a book about birds?* _____

2 *Tell me more, please!* _____

3 *Can you write your name for me in my book?* _____

4 *Sorry, I can't come to the park now. I want to finish my maths.* _____

5 *Hey, that one looks just like a cow.* _____

GRAMMAR
like + -ing

1 **Look at the sentences from the blog on page 16. Draw 🙂 or ☹ next to each one.**

   1 I love collecting autographs. _____
   2 I can't stand walking to school. _____
   3 I hate being on my own. _____
   4 I like writing poems. _____

2 **Use the sentences in Exercise 1 to complete the rule.**

> **RULE:** Use the ¹_____ form of the verb after verbs which express likes and dislikes, e.g. *like, love, hate, enjoy, can't stand*.
> * To make this form add ²_____ to the base verb.
> * If the verb ends in -e, drop the final -e (e.g. *live – living*).
> * If a short verb ends in a consonant + vowel + consonant, we usually double the final consonant before adding the -ing (e.g. *swim – swimming*).

3 **Complete the sentences. Use the -ing form of the verbs in the list.**

~~run~~ | visit | swim | eat | ride | talk

   0 I hate _running_ to catch the bus to school.
   1 My mum and dad enjoy _____ in nice restaurants.
   2 My brother can't stand _____ on the telephone.
   3 They quite like _____ in the sea when it's warm.
   4 Donna really likes _____ her horse.
   5 We love _____ new places on holiday.

4 **WRITING** What about you? Write two or three sentences about yourself.

Adverbs of frequency

5 **Complete the diagram with the words in the list.**

always | occasionally | never | often

6 **Complete the sentences so they are true for you.**

   1 I _____ do my homework when I get home.
   2 I _____ write 'thank you' cards for my presents.
   3 I am _____ late for school.
   4 I _____ watch TV in the mornings.
   5 Mum is _____ angry if I don't tidy my room.
   6 I _____ turn off the lights when I leave the room.

7 **Complete these sentences from the blog on page 16. Check your answers and complete the rule.**

   1 _____ _____ _____ my granddad takes me out for a milkshake.
   2 I watch it (the TV news) _____ _____ .

> **RULE:** Words like *sometimes*, *never*, *always* come ¹*before* / *after* the verb *to be* but ²*before* / *after* other verbs.
> Phrases like *every day* or *twice a week* can come at the beginning or at the end of a sentence.

8 **Write down things you do …**

   every day: _I give my mum a kiss every day._
   three times a week: _____
   once a year: _____

9 **SPEAKING** Work in small groups. Compare your answers to Exercises 6 and 8.

> *How often do you go to the cinema?*

> *I go once a month …*

> Workbook page 11 →

WRITING
Your routine

Complete the sentences so they are true for you.

1 I rarely _____ at the weekend.
2 I can't stand _____ .
3 I _____ three times every day.
4 I love _____ in August.
5 I never _____ when I'm tired.
6 I _____ once a week.
7 I occasionally _____ .
8 I enjoy _____ after school.

Adverbs of frequency

0% ——————————————————————————————— 100%

¹_____ rarely ²_____ sometimes ³_____ usually ⁴_____

Olivia's new hobby

1 Look at the photos and answer the questions.

What do you think Olivia's hobby is?
Why does Ryan look worried?

2 🔊 1.21 Now read and listen to the photostory.
Check your answers.

LUKE Look. It's Olivia and Megan.
RYAN What are they up to?
LUKE I'm not sure what they're doing but
they're definitely having a good time.
RYAN Let's go and find out.

OLIVIA Hi, Ryan. Hi, Luke.
RYAN Hi, Olivia. So what are you two doing?
OLIVIA It's my new hobby. I take photos of Megan
reading a book in strange places.
LUKE Cool! Can I video you on my phone?
OLIVIA Of course you can. Come on.

LUKE This is great. I think I've got a new hobby
too – making videos.
RYAN Be careful, Luke. Don't push too hard.
OLIVIA That's right. Be careful.
MEGAN Don't stop, Luke. I'm having fun.

OLIVIA That's great, Megan.
MEGAN Hurry up. My arms are tired.
I need to have a rest.
OLIVIA Just a few more.
RYAN Look out, Olivia! You're very close
to the water.

DEVELOPING SPEAKING

3 Work in pairs. Discuss what happens next in the story. Write down your ideas.

We think Olivia falls in the water.

4 ▶ **EP1** Watch to find out how the story continues.

5 (Circle) the correct word in each sentence.

0 Ryan (tries) / *doesn't try* to warn Olivia.

1 Ryan and Luke *help* / *don't help* her out of the water.

2 Olivia *cries* / *doesn't cry* when she falls into the water.

3 Olivia *laughs* / *doesn't laugh* when she sees her camera.

4 Her camera *is* / *isn't* broken.

5 Luke *tells* / *doesn't tell* them what the surprise is.

6 Luke *gives* / *doesn't give* Olivia the money.

PHRASES FOR FLUENCY

1 Find the expressions 1–5 in the photostory. Who says them? Match them to the definitions a–f.

0 (What are they) up to? _Ryan_ | e |

1 Cool! _____ | |

2 Come on. _____ | |

3 That's right. _____ | |

4 Hurry up. _____ | |

5 Look out! _____ | |

a Be quick. **d** Let's start.

b Correct. **e** Doing.

c Be careful. **f** Great.

2 Complete the conversation with the expressions in Exercise 1.

In the park

SARAH Hi, Nancy. What are you ⁰ _up to_ ?

NICOLE Not a lot. Just walking. Are you here for a walk too?

SARAH ¹ _____ . I'm a bit bored at home.

NICOLE Me too. We can walk together, if you want.

SARAH ² _____ ! Oh no – ³ _____ ! Mike Smith is coming. I don't like him!

NICOLE ⁴ _____ – let's walk over here.

SARAH I don't want him to see me. ⁵ _____ , Nancy!

Workbook page 12 ➜

WordWise
Collocations with *have*

1 Match the sentence parts from the story.

1 ☐ I'm not sure what they're doing

2 ☐ Don't stop, Luke.

3 ☐ You're really dirty. You need to go home

4 ☐ My arms are tired.

5 ☐ Olivia, I think you *have a problem*.

6 ☐ We're just *having dinner*.

a I'm *having fun*.

b I think your camera's broken.

c It's pizza. Would you like some?

d I need to *have a rest*.

e but they're definitely *having a good time*.

f and *have a shower*.

2 Ask and answer the questions in pairs.

1 Who do you have the most fun with?

2 Do you have a good time at school?

3 What do you do when you have a problem?

4 What time do you have dinner?

5 Do you have a rest after school?

6 When do you have a shower?

FUNCTIONS
Giving warnings and stating prohibition

1 Put the words in order to make sentences.

1 Dan / Be / careful **3** do / that / Don't

2 out / Lucy / Look **4** push / Don't / hard / too

2 Match the sentences in Exercise 1 with the pictures A–D.

2 MONEY AND HOW TO SPEND IT

OBJECTIVES

FUNCTIONS: buying things in a shop; talking about what people are doing at the moment
GRAMMAR: present continuous; verbs of perception; present simple vs. present continuous
VOCABULARY: shops; clothes

READING

1 🔊 1.22 Say these prices. Listen and check.

PRICE €1.49 — 1
£22.75 — 2
$249.00 — 3
£5.99 — 4
$8.25 — 5
£835.00 — 6

2 🔊 1.23 What are these objects? Match them with the prices in Exercise 1. Write 1–6 in the boxes. Listen and check.

3 SPEAKING Work in pairs. Discuss the following questions. Then compare your ideas with other students.

Which of the things in Exercise 2 do you …
1 think are cheap?
2 think are expensive?
3 think are fantastic?
4 dream about having?

4 Look at the picture on page 21. Answer these questions.
1 Who do you think the boy and girl are?
2 Do you think the girl likes the shirt?

5 🔊 1.24 Read and listen to the script from a soap opera and check your ideas.

6 Mark the sentences T (true) or F (false). Correct the false ones.
0 It's six o'clock on Friday afternoon.
   It's four o'clock on Friday afternoon.
1 Tom is deciding what to wear.
2 Maddy thinks yellow is a good idea.
3 Tom thinks he's good-looking.
4 Tom wants to buy expensive clothes.
5 Tom wants to be famous.

A
B
C
D
E
F

TOM	Hi, Maddy.
MADDY	Where are Mum and Dad?
TOM	They're out. At the supermarket, I think. They're doing some shopping or something.
MADDY	What are you doing?
TOM	Me? I'm looking for something.
MADDY	OK. What are you looking for?
TOM	A shirt. And some trousers. I'm going out. It's Friday and I have plans for tonight. So, I'm choosing my clothes.
MADDY	But it's only four o'clock.
TOM	I know. I need time to choose.
MADDY	Do you need any help? I can help you.
TOM	No. Well, maybe. OK, yes.
MADDY	Think about colours.
TOM	I'm thinking. I'm thinking about … yellow.
MADDY	Not a good idea.
TOM	Why not?
MADDY	Because yellow just isn't interesting.
TOM	But I like yellow. Like this.
MADDY	I'm trying to help you, Tom. And I'm telling you – don't wear a yellow shirt.
TOM	You're laughing. Why are you laughing at me?
MADDY	I'm not laughing at you. I'm laughing at the shirt. It looks terrible.
TOM	I need some new ideas.
MADDY	You're right. Look at this. Here, in this magazine. See this guy? He's wearing beautiful clothes.
TOM	Yes, but he's good-looking. And rich too, probably. I'm not good-looking.
MADDY	Yes, you are! But of course, I'm only saying that because you're my brother. OK, have you got your money?
TOM	Yes. Why?
MADDY	I want to take you to town – to a clothes shop and maybe a shoe shop, too.
TOM	That sounds great. Nothing expensive though.
MADDY	Don't worry. Nice clothes aren't always expensive. Come on.
TOM	You know, I dream about being famous one day and about having fantastic clothes. Do you dream about that too?
MADDY	Tom, I'm nine years old. I dream about ice cream.
TOM	OK, we can get ice cream after we buy the clothes.

■ THiNK VALUES ■

Fashion and clothes

1   How important are these for you? Give each one a number from 0 to 5 (0 = not important, 5 = very, very important).

Clothes – my values:

- [ ] I want to look cool.
- [ ] I want to feel comfortable.
- [ ] I always buy cheap clothes.
- [ ] I like buying designer clothes.
- [ ] I love wearing clean clothes.
- [ ] I like wearing bright colours.
- [ ] I always buy clothes in the same shops.

2   **SPEAKING** Work in pairs. Ask and answer questions.

> *How important is it for you to look cool?*

> *Not very important. I have 3 points. What about you?*

> *For me, it's very important. 5 points.*

GRAMMAR
Present continuous

1 **Look at the examples of the present continuous. Then complete the rule and the table.**

1 They**'re doing** some shopping at the supermarket.
2 He**'s wearing** beautiful clothes.
3 Why **are** you **laughing** at me?
4 I**'m not laughing** at you, Tom.

> **RULE:** Use the present ¹_____ to talk about things that are happening at or around the time of speaking.
> Form the present continuous with the present simple of ²_____ + the *-ing* form (e.g. *running* / *doing* / *wearing*, etc.) of the main verb.

Positive	Negative
I'm (= I am) working.	I'm not working.
you/we/they're (¹_____) working.	you/we/they aren't working.
he/she/it's (is) working.	he/she/it ²_____ working.

Questions	Short answers
³_____ I working?	Yes, I am. No, I'm not.
⁴_____ you/we/they working?	Yes, you/we/they ⁶_____ . No, you/we/they ⁷_____ .
⁵_____ he/she/it working?	Yes, he/she/it ⁸_____ . No, he/she/it ⁹_____ .

2 **Complete the sentences. Use the present continuous of the verbs.**

0 Sorry, Jenny's not here. She *'s doing* (do) some shopping in town.
1 They're in the living room. They _____ (play) computer games.
2 My brother's in the garage. He _____ (clean) his bike.
3 Steven! You _____ (not listen) to me!
4 I can't talk now. I _____ (do) my homework.
5 It's 3–0! We _____ (not play) very well, and we _____ (lose)!
6 A _____ you _____ (watch) this programme?
   B No, I _____ . You can watch a different one if you want.
7 A What _____ you _____ (do)?
   B I _____ (try) to find some old photos on my computer.

Workbook page 18

VOCABULARY
Shops

1 **Write the names of the shops under the photos.**

newsagent's | chemist's | bookshop
clothes shop | shoe shop | department store
supermarket | sports shop

1 _____

2 _____

3 _____

4 _____

5 _____

6 _____

7 _____

8 _____

2 **SPEAKING Complete the sentences with the names of shops from Exercise 1. Then compare your ideas with other students.**

1 In my town there's a very good …
   It's called … It's good because …
2 I often go there because …
3 I never go into … because they don't interest me. I don't often go to … because …

> *In my town there's a very good clothes shop.*
> *It's good because the clothes aren't expensive.*

Workbook page 20

GRAMMAR
Verbs of perception

1 **Look at the sentences from the script on page 21. Answer the questions.**

  1 *It looks terrible.*   What is 'it'?
  2 *That sounds great.*   What is 'that'?

2 **Match the verbs with the pictures. Then complete the rule.**

  1 look   2 sound   3 smell   4 taste

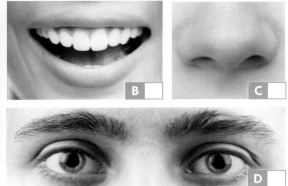
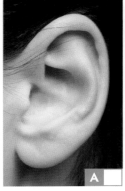

> **RULE:** Verbs of perception are used in the present [1]_____ when they are used to give an opinion.
>
> *The food **tastes** great.*   *That idea **sounds** good.*   *That pizza **smells** nice.*   *His new shirt **looks** awful!*
>
> The words after the verbs of perception are [2]_____.

3 **Match the responses (a–d) to the first parts of the conversations (1–4).**

  1 I'm going to the cinema.   ☐
  2 My mother's making pizzas.   ☐
  3 I'm wearing my new shoes.   ☐
  4 Don't you like the juice?   ☐

  a No. It tastes horrible!   c They smell fantastic.
  b That sounds great.   d They look nice.

> **Workbook page 19** ➡

LISTENING

1 🔊**1.25** **Listen. What shop is each person in? Write numbers.**

  ☐ bookshop   ☐ newsagent's
  ☐ clothes shop   ☐ sports shop

2 🔊**1.25** **Listen again. What does each person want to buy?**

  1 _____   3 _____
  2 _____   4 _____

FUNCTIONS
Buying things in a shop

1 **Read the sentences from the listening. Mark them C (customer) or A (assistant).**

  0 Can I help you?   *A*
  1 Have you got … ?   ☐
  2 What size do you take?   ☐
  3 Can I try it/them on please?   ☐
  4 How much is it/are they?   ☐
  5 That's (twenty pounds) please.   ☐
  6 Have you got it/them in (blue)?   ☐

2 🔊**1.26** **Put the sentences in the correct order 1–9. Listen and check. Practise in pairs.**

  ☐ A It's £75.00.
  1 A Hello. Can I help you?
  ☐ A Great. So – that's £75, please!
  ☐ A Sorry, no. Only brown.
  ☐ A Yes, of course.
  ☐ B Can I try it on?
  ☐ B Very nice. I'll take it.
  ☐ B Yes, please. I like this jacket. Have you got it in black?
  ☐ B Oh, well, brown's OK. How much is it?

ROLE PLAY **Buying clothes in a shop**

Work in pairs. Student A: Go to page 127. Student B: Go to page 128. Take two or three minutes to prepare. Then have two conversations.

■ TRAIN TO THiNK ■
Exploring numbers

1 **You want to buy some new clothes. Here are some things you like. Answer the questions in pairs.**

  T-Shirt – £8.50   shoes – £12.75   jumper – £9.25
  belt – £3   jacket – £35

  1 Choose three things. How much do they cost?
  2 You've got £30.00. Name three things you can buy.
  3 You've got £75.00. Can you buy all five things?

2 **SPEAKING** **Compare your ideas with a partner.**

> **Pronunciation**
> Contractions
> **Go to page 120.** 🔊

VOCABULARY
Clothes

1 🔊 1.29 **Complete the names of the clothes. Listen and check.**

0 _b_ e _l_ _t_	5 __ oo __ __
1 __ __ e __ __	6 __ a __ __ e __
2 __ u __ __ e __	7 __ __ i __ __
3 __ __ oe __	8 __ __ o __ __ __ __
4 __ __ ai __ e __ __	9 __ __ ou __ e __ __

2 **Answer the questions.**

1 What are you wearing now?
2 What do you usually wear at the weekends?
3 What do you never wear?
4 What clothes do you really like / dislike buying?

3 **SPEAKING** Work in pairs. Ask and answer the questions in Exercise 2. Then work with another partner.

> *I'm wearing a green shirt and jeans.*

> *I never wear shorts.*

Workbook page 20

READING

1 **Read the web chat. Answer the questions.**

Who …

1 is interested in the sky?
2 is probably in the kitchen?
3 has a problem?
4 is in front of a TV?
5 is surprising her parents?

2 **Think of three things you enjoy that don't need money. Write them down.**
going for a walk   watching TV

3 **SPEAKING** Work in pairs. Tell your partner your ideas. Listen to what your partner says. Are his/her ideas really things that don't need money? Say what you think.

> *I like going for a walk. I also like watching TV.*

> *I like baking cakes.*

> *But you need money to buy ingredients!*

How not to spend money   ✕

😃 **JollyMarie**
5 June 2015

Wow! Problem. Not a lot of money right now and I don't want to spend it. I'm tired of spending money! So here I am at home and I'm thinking – what can I do that's free? (and fun lol)

👍👎 **LIKE • COMMENT • SHARE**

goodgirl
an hour ago

I always go into town at the weekend – and I usually spend money! It's very easy to buy things if you go into a shopping mall or a street full of shops. So this weekend I'm staying at home. Right now I'm just reading a book – my parents can't believe it! lol

PeteJ
yesterday

I really like going to the cinema but it can be a bit expensive – especially because my friends and I often go for a pizza after the film. So tonight I'm watching a film on TV at home. I'm really enjoying it. And it's free! It's incredible how many good films there are on TV these days, too.

RonnieRaver
two days ago

It's funny, PeteJ – I'm just like you (going to the cinema, I mean). Right now, I'm not watching a film – I'm watching the stars! I've got a book about the sky and it's fantastic. I'm having a really good time here!

EllieParsons
two days ago

Oh JollyMarie, it's not such a problem. My friends and I often have a picnic on Sundays and I make the sandwiches the night before. So right now, it's Saturday night and I'm making sandwiches. hehehe

GRAMMAR
Present simple vs. present continuous

1 Look at the examples. Complete the rule.

present simple
I usually **watch** a film at the cinema.
I **make** the sandwiches the night before.
I always **go** into town.

present continuous
Right now, I**'m watching** a film.
It's Saturday night and I**'m making** sandwiches.
This weekend, I**'m staying** at home.

> **RULE:** Use the ¹_____ to talk about habits, routines and things which are generally or always true.
> Use the ²_____ to talk about temporary things which are happening around the moment of speaking.

2 Match the sentences with the pictures. Write 1–4 in the boxes.

1 She sings well.
2 She's singing well.
3 He plays football.
4 He's playing football.

 A

 B

 C

 D

> **LOOK!** These verbs are almost never used in the present continuous:
>
> believe | know | understand | mean
> remember | need | like | hate | want
>
> *I **know** the answer.* (Not: ~~I'm knowing the answer.~~)
> *I **understand** the problem.* (Not: ~~I am understanding the problem.~~)

3 Circle the correct options.

1 We *always wear* / *'re always wearing* a uniform to school.
2 Paula *wears* / *is wearing* black jeans today.
3 Come inside! It *rains* / *'s raining*.
4 It *rains* / *'s raining* a lot in February.
5 Dad *cooks* / *'s cooking* at the moment.
6 My mother *cooks* / *'s cooking* lunch every Sunday.
7 Steve's terrible! He *never listens* / *'s never listening* to the teacher!
8 Can you be quiet, please? I *listen* / *'m listening* to some music.

4 Complete the sentences. Use the present simple or present continuous form of the verbs.

0 Mandy usually __*goes*__ (go) to school on her bike, but today she __*is walking*__ (walk).
1 We _____ (have) science lessons three times a week. This week we _____ (learn) about trees.
2 Tom _____ (do) some shopping this afternoon. He _____ (want) to buy a new camera.
3 I _____ (know) her face, but I _____ (not remember) her name.
4 Alex _____ (not watch) the game tonight because he _____ (not like) football very much.
5 What _____ this word _____ (mean)? I _____ (not understand) it.

> Workbook page 19 ➤

SPEAKING

1 Look at these photos. Who are the people in each one?

2 Work in pairs. Discuss the questions.

For each person, say …
● who they are.
● what they do.
● what they are doing.

> *It's Beyoncé. She's a …*
> *She's …*

Culture

1 **Look at the photos. Name one or two things you can buy in each market.**
- Where can you see stalls?
- Where can you see a canal?

2 🔊 **1.30 Read and listen to the article. Match the photos with the places. Write the numbers 1–5 in the boxes.**

A

World markets

Wherever you go in the world, you find shops and stores – but you can find wonderful markets in most cities, too. Here's a selection from five different countries.

1 The **Spice Bazaar** in **Istanbul** is popular with both tourists and people from Istanbul. There are lots of shops and stalls and they all sell many different kinds of spices, sweets or nuts. You can buy spices from a lot of countries (like Iran, China, Russia and of course Turkey), and the smells and colours are amazing.

2 **Khlong Lat Phli** is a very unusual market about 80 kilometres south of **Bangkok**, Thailand. Early every morning, hundreds of local people sell fruit and vegetables from their boats on the canals. It's not the only boat market in the country but it's a very popular tourist one.

3 Do you like fish? Then the **Tsukiji Market** in **Tokyo** is the right place for you. It is the biggest seafood market in the world, and

it never closes! It's very busy between the hours of 4.00 and 5.00 am, when people from the shops and restaurants in Tokyo buy the fresh fish that they need for the day. It is also very popular with tourists, but they can only visit the market later in the day, after the early morning buying and selling.

4 In **Madrid** there is a famous open-air market called **El Rastro**, which is open on Sunday mornings. There are over 1,000 stalls that sell many different things: books, CDs, paintings, antiques – beautiful old things. One of the streets sells only animals and birds. And of course visitors can stop to eat 'tapas' and get something to drink, and there are many street musicians with their guitars making music too.

C

5 **Portobello Road Market** in **London** is popular with tourists and with Londoners, too. You can find all kinds of bargains here. The market (in Notting Hill) has five different parts and you can buy new or second-hand things (like clothes) as well as fruit and vegetables, and antiques. It's very busy at the weekend.

D

E

3 **VOCABULARY** There are eight highlighted words in the article. Match the words with these meanings. Write the words.

0 big tables or small shops with an open front *stalls*

1 not inside a building _____

2 fish and other things to eat from the sea _____

3 different or surprising _____

4 small man-made rivers _____

5 full of people _____

6 liked by a lot of people _____

7 things that you buy for a good, cheap price _____

4 Read the article again. Correct the information in these sentences.

0 All the spices at the Istanbul Spice Bazaar are from Turkey.
Not all the spices are from Turkey. You can buy spices from a lot of countries.

1 At Khlong Lat Phli, people sell spices from their boats.

2 The Tsukiji Market closes between four and five in the morning.

3 Tourists can go to the Tsukiji Market in the early morning.

4 You can't get food at El Rastro.

5 Portobello Road Market is very quiet on Saturdays.

SPEAKING

1 Make sentences about the markets that are true for you. Use adjectives from the list, or other adjectives if you want.

fantastic | interesting | fascinating
exciting | unusual | attractive

I think the ... market is fantastic / isn't very interesting because ...

2 Work in groups. Compare your sentences and ideas.

> *I think the Istanbul Spice market is fantastic because ...*

WRITING
An email to say what you're doing

1 Read the email from Paul to his friend Lucy. Answer the questions.

1 Where is Paul and what is he doing?

2 Where are his father and sister?

3 What is Paul's family watching tonight?

2 How does Paul start his email? And how does he finish it? Complete the table with the words in the list.

Dear | Love | Hello | See you soon | Best wishes

starting an email	ending an email
Hi (Lucy), 1 _____ (Mike) 2 _____ (Mr Jones)	Hope you are OK. Bye 3 _____ 4 _____ 5 _____

3 Look at paragraphs 1 and 2 of Paul's email. Match the functions with the paragraphs. Write a–d.

Paragraph 1: _____ and _____ .
Paragraph 2: _____ and _____ .

a saying what you are doing

b talking about your plans

c saying where you are

d a description of the place where you are

4 Tick (✓) the things Paul writes about in his email.

1 what he likes about the city ☐

2 when he is coming home ☐

3 his plans for tonight ☐

4 where he is staying ☐

5 what his mother/father/sister are doing ☐

6 how Lucy is ☐

5 Write an email to a friend (about 100–120 words). Imagine you are in a café or shop in a shopping centre. Use the example email and language above to help you.

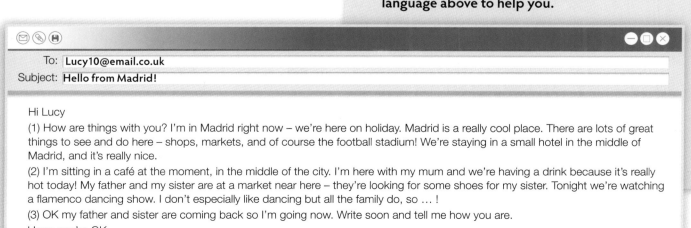

To: Lucy10@email.co.uk
Subject: Hello from Madrid!

Hi Lucy

(1) How are things with you? I'm in Madrid right now – we're here on holiday. Madrid is a really cool place. There are lots of great things to see and do here – shops, markets, and of course the football stadium! We're staying in a small hotel in the middle of Madrid, and it's really nice.

(2) I'm sitting in a café at the moment, in the middle of the city. I'm here with my mum and we're having a drink because it's really hot today! My father and my sister are at a market near here – they're looking for some shoes for my sister. Tonight we're watching a flamenco dancing show. I don't especially like dancing but all the family do, so … !

(3) OK my father and sister are coming back so I'm going now. Write soon and tell me how you are.

Hope you're OK.

Paul

CAMBRIDGE ENGLISH: Key

THiNK EXAMS

READING AND WRITING
Part 3: Multiple-choice replies

Workbook page 17

1 **Complete the five conversations. Choose the correct answer A, B or C.**

0 What are you doing?
   A I play computer games.
   B I'm a doctor.
   C I'm trying to find my school bag. *(circled)*

1 How often are you late for school?
   A on Mondays
   B about once a month
   C at ten o'clock

2 Does your brother go to your school?
   A Yes, he does go.
   B Yes, he goes.
   C Yes, he does.

3 What do you think of my new haircut?
   A It looks really good.
   B It's looking really good.
   C It sounds great.

4 Do you like doing puzzles?
   A Yes, I like.
   B Three times a week.
   C No, I can't stand them.

5 Do you live in a big town?
   A No, we aren't.
   B Yes, we do.
   C No, you don't.

Part 6: Word completion

Workbook page 43

2 **Read the descriptions of clothes. What is the word for each one? The first letter is already there. There is one space for each other letter in the word.**

0 You can wear this over your shirt when you go out.
   j *a c k e t*

1 Wear these shoes to play sport. **t** _ _ _ _ _ _ _ _

2 Put this on if it's cold. **j** _ _ _ _ _ _

3 Some boys wear trousers to school, other boys wear these. **s** _ _ _ _ _ _

4 You wear this around the top of your trousers.
   b _ _ _ _

5 A lot of teenagers wear these. **j** _ _ _ _ _

LISTENING
Part 1: Multiple-choice pictures

Workbook page 25

3 🔊 1.31 **You will hear five short conversations. There is one question for each conversation. For each question, choose the right answer (A, B or C).**

0 What are the girls talking about?

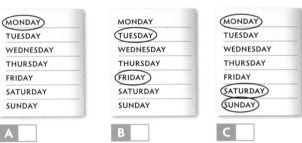

A ☐   B ✓   C ☐

1 When does Oliver play tennis?

A ☐   B ☐   C ☐

2 Where is Brian?

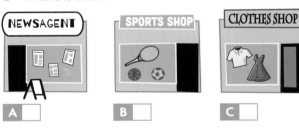

A ☐   B ☐   C ☐

3 What is Molly's hobby?

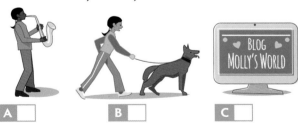

A ☐   B ☐   C ☐

4 How much is the red jumper?

A ☐   B ☐   C ☐

TEST YOURSELF

VOCABULARY

1 **Complete the sentences with the words in the list. There are two extra words.**

newsagent's | take | dress | club | write | plays | collects
sports shop | supermarket | jumper | shoe shop | belt

1 I want to _____ a blog about pop music.
2 If you're cold, why don't you put on a _____?
3 She _____ the guitar and the piano. She's really good at both.
4 I need to go to the _____ and buy some tennis balls.
5 My dad _____ old toy cars. He's just a big child!
6 You need some new boots. Let's go to the _____ .
7 I'm thinking about joining the golf _____ but it's very expensive.
8 Your trousers are falling down. You need a _____ .
9 Can you get some eggs and some milk when you go to the _____ , please?
10 I always _____ lots of photos when I travel.

/10

GRAMMAR

2 **Complete the sentences with the words in the list.**

's working | 're writing | works | plays | 're playing | write

1 My dad's a cook. He _____ at a restaurant in town.
2 I like poetry. I _____ at least five poems every week.
3 Mum's in her office. She _____ on something very important.
4 Paul's in a band. He _____ the drums.
5 Ian and Dan are on the computer. They _____ their blog.
6 Lucy and Rachel are in the garden. They _____ football.

3 **Find and correct the mistake in each sentence.**

1 I can't stand to eat carrots.
2 We don't playing very well today.
3 They doesn't like playing video games.
4 That sandwich is tasting very good.
5 Does you speak French?
6 He goes always swimming at the weekend.

/12

FUNCTIONAL LANGUAGE

4 **Write the missing words.**

1 A Be _____ ! It looks very dangerous.
   B Don't worry. I'm _____ fun.
2 A How _____ do you watch TV?
   B _____ day when I get home from school.
3 A Look _____ ! There's a dog coming.
   B And it _____ look happy. Let's run!
4 A Please _____ shout! The baby is asleep.
   B Oh, OK. I'm _____ .

/8

MY SCORE [____] /30

| 22 – 30 |
| 10 – 21 |
| 0 – 9 |

3 | FOOD FOR LIFE

OBJECTIVES

FUNCTIONS: apologising; talking about food; ordering a meal

GRAMMAR: countable and uncountable nouns; *a/an, some, any; How much / many, a lot of / lots of ; too* and *(not) enough*

VOCABULARY: food and drink; adjectives to talk about food; expressions with *have got*

A bread

READING

1 What food and drink in the picture can you name? What food and drink do you know in English?

2 Make sentences that are true for you. Compare your ideas in class.

| I | always often sometimes never | have … for | breakfast. lunch. dinner. |

3 Look at the photos on page 31. Ask your teacher for the words you don't know. Then answer the questions.

> What's … in English?

Can you think of a food that …

- comes from another country?
- has got a lot of vitamins?
- is very healthy?
- is unusual?
- is good for your hair and skin?

4 ◀)) 1.32 Read and listen to the article. Match the parts of the sentences.

0	In Japan people think square watermelons	*e*
1	Bananas are a popular fruit because they	
2	In Iceland people don't like	
3	Honey is healthy and good	
4	Avocado is a dessert in	
5	Potato clocks are very popular in	
6	Sugar is not only in sweets. It's also in	

a 'normal' ice creams.
b Brazil.
c for our looks.
d West Africa.

e make very special presents.
f fruit.
g help us feel good.

5 **SPEAKING** Work in pairs. Three of the 'food facts' in Exercise 4 are not true. Which ones do you think they are?

> I don't think that people give square watermelons as special presents in Japan.

> I think it's true that …

> Yes, you're right. I think so too. / No, I think that's impossible.

> What do you think about statement number …?

> I'm not sure. I think … Do you agree?

> Yes, I do. / No, I don't. I think …

Food Facts or Food Fiction?

In Japan, square watermelons are very popular. People often buy them as presents. But these special fruits are of course very expensive. Round watermelons do not cost so much.

People all over the world love bananas. Food experts say that bananas contain a chemical that helps the body to produce serotonin. It's sometimes called the body's own 'happiness hormone'.

People in Iceland love eating unusual ice creams. There is pizza ice cream, sausage ice cream and even fish and chips ice cream, and they are all very popular. People eat them with a lot of ketchup. But you don't find any lemon or mango ice creams there. Icelanders just don't like them.

Honey is very healthy. It has got lots of vitamins. Some people say that honey makes us beautiful. They think it's good for the hair and the skin. Honey is also very special because it is the only food we eat that never goes off. We can eat 3,000- or 4,000-year-old honey!

The avocado is a fruit, not a vegetable. It comes from Central and South America originally, but now it also grows in other hot countries. Many people like avocados as a starter before their main meal. But how many people eat it as a dessert? Well, in Brazil, people eat avocado with ice cream and milk.

People in West Africa use a 'potato-clock' to tell the time. Every morning, they put exactly 7.5 kilos of potatoes in the clock. It looks like a big pot. They put it on the fire. They know that it takes two hours to cook the potatoes.

Everybody knows that fruit has got sugar in it. But how much sugar is there in a lemon? A lot. More than there is in a strawberry!

■ THiNK VALUES ■

Food and health

1 Complete the five conversations. Choose the correct answer A, B or C.

1 Do you want some ice cream?
   A No, thanks. Can I have an apple or a banana?
   B She's not hungry.
   C They're very good.

2 Have some water.
   A I drink it.
   B No, thanks, I'm not thirsty.
   C Look at them.

3 Would you like more chocolate?
   A It's over there.
   B Yes, I do.
   C I'd love some, but I'm trying not to eat too much.

4 Do you eat any vegetables?
   A I hate apples.
   B It's fast food.
   C No, I don't. I don't like them.

5 Have some biscuits.
   A Thanks, but one's enough for me.
   B You can have a banana.
   C I'm very healthy.

2 SPEAKING Work in pairs. Compare your answers. Do the people care about healthy food?

The person in number 1	doesn't want a ...	He/She asks for ...
	likes ...	He/She says ...
	never eats / drinks ...	He/She wants ...

| I think he/she | cares about ... |
| | doesn't care about ... |

VOCABULARY
Food and drink

1 🔊 1.33 Write the names of the food under the pictures. Listen and check.

1

2

3

4

5

6

7

8

9

10

2 **SPEAKING** Work in pairs. Ask and answer questions to find out three things your partner likes and doesn't like.

Workbook page 30

GRAMMAR
Countable and uncountable nouns

1 Read the sentences. Then (circle) the correct words in the rule.

1 Can I have a carrot?
2 I don't like rice.
3 I don't like peppers.

> **RULE:** Nouns that you can count (*one carrot, two carrots*, etc.) are [1]*countable / uncountable* nouns.
>
> Nouns you cannot count are [2]*countable / uncountable* nouns. They have no plural forms.

2 Look at the photos in Exercise 1. Which are countable and which are uncountable?

a/an, some, any

3 Complete the sentences with *a/an*, *some* and *any*. Then (circle) the correct words in the rule.

1 A Would you like _____ water?
  B No, thanks. I've got _____ tea.
2 Can I have _____ apple or _____ banana?
3 Have _____ biscuits.
4 Are there _____ vegetables in the kitchen?
5 There isn't _____ milk in the fridge.

> **RULE:** Use *a/an* with [1]*singular / plural* countable nouns.
>
> Use *some* with [2]*singular / plural* countable and uncountable nouns.
>
> Use *any* in questions and in [3]*positive / negative* sentences.
>
> Use *some* in questions when offering or requesting something.

4 Complete the sentences with *a/an*, *some* and *any*.

1 A Would you like _____ vegetables?
  B No, thanks. I don't like _____ vegetables.
2 A I'd like _____ strawberries, please.
  B Strawberries? Yes, I think we have _____ .
3 I'd like _____ tomatoes.
4 I don't want _____ coffee.
5 Can I have _____ orange, please?
6 Do you want _____ sugar in your tea?

(how much) / (how) many / a lot of / lots of

5 Look at the examples. Complete the rule.

How much sugar is there in a lemon?	**How many** people eat avocado as a dessert?
I don't eat **much** chocolate.	We haven't got **many** apples.
Bananas have got **a lot of** sugar.	**A lot of** people like avocados.
Watermelons have got **lots of** water.	Honey has got **lots of** vitamins.

> **RULE:** We typically use *(How) much* and *(How) many* in **questions** and **negative** sentences.
> Use *many* with **plural** 1_____ nouns and *much* with 2_____ nouns.
> Use *a lot of / lots of* with both **countable** and **uncountable** 3_____ .

6 (Circle) the correct words in questions 1–6. Then match them with the answers a–f.

1 ☐ How *much / many* apples do you want?
2 ☐ How *much / many* sugar is there in an avocado?
3 ☐ Are there *much / many* boys in your class?
4 ☐ How *much / many* peppers are there?
5 ☐ How *much / many* time have you got?
6 ☐ Have you got *many / a lot of* homework?

a I think there are about five.
b Just one, please.
c Only 10 minutes.
d No, I haven't got any.
e I have no idea. I don't think it's a lot.
f Yes, there are 12, and 5 girls. `Workbook page 28`

LISTENING

1 🔊 1.34 Complete the menu with words from the list. Listen and check.

cheesecake | chips | tomato | onion rings | chicken spinach and mushroom | hot chocolate | fruit

BLUES CAFÉ MENU

OUR DELICIOUS STARTERS
1_____ soup
mushroom soup
2_____ omelette
ham and cheese omelette

LUNCH SPECIALS
steak
grilled 3_____
pasta with tomatoes

SIDE DISHES
4_____
5_____
mixed salad

DESSERTS
yoghurt and strawberries
vanilla and chocolate ice cream
6_____

DRINKS
7_____ juices
mineral water
8_____
tea
coffee

2 🔊 1.35 Jane and Sam are in the Blues Café. Listen and find out who eats more. Listen again and complete the sentences below.

1 Jane wants the …
2 Sam orders …
3 He doesn't want …

3 🔊 1.35 Complete the sentences with *get, menu, drink, we'd, some* and *bill*. Then listen again and check.

Waiter: | Customer:
Can I help you? → | 1_____ like something to eat. Thanks.
Here's the 2_____ . ← |
What would you like to 3_____ ? → | An orange juice for me, please.
I'll be right back. ← | And for me 4_____ mineral water, please
What can I 5_____ you? → | I'd like the spinach and mushroom omelette.
Would you like a starter? → | Yes, please. Can I have the … , please? / No, thanks.
| Can we have the 6_____ , please?
Of course. That's £ … . | Here you are.
Thank you. Bye, bye / Thanks very much. ← | Thank you. Bye.

4 **SPEAKING** Work in groups. One is the waiter, the others are customers. Order meals. Use the menu in Exercise 1 and the conversations in Exercise 3.

■ THiNK SELF-ESTEEM ■

Being happy

1 Read these statements. Tick (✓) the ones that you think are important for being happy. Write a cross (✗) against the ones that you think are not so important.

1 There's no 'right' body shape or size. Healthy and happy people come in all shapes and sizes. ☐
2 You can only find out what kind of person someone is if you get to know them better. ☐
3 Never laugh about people for being too thin, too short, too tall or too fat. ☐
4 Never laugh at other people's jokes about people's looks. That's unfair and it hurts. ☐
5 Being thin is not the same as being healthy and happy. ☐
6 Like yourself for who you are and for the things you are good at. ☐

2 **SPEAKING** Work in pairs. Say what you think is important for being happy.

Pronunciation
Vowel sounds: /ɪ/ and /iː/
Go to page 120. 🔊

READING

1 **Look at Jenny's blog for not more than 15 seconds and answer the questions. Then read and check your answers.**

1 How old is Jenny?
2 How is she feeling?
3 What's the problem?

2 **Read the blog again. Answer the questions.**

1 How do Jenny's parents react to Jeremy's cooking?
2 What does Jeremy sometimes do with the food his family don't eat?
3 Why does Jeremy sing when he serves his spaghetti?
4 What does Jenny like about the meals Jeremy serves?
5 Why does Jenny say that her mum and dad's dance class is 'unhealthy'?

WRITING
Your favourite meal

1 **Put the sentences or phrases in order to make an email from Jenny to her friend.**

a		Actually this week it's not a surprise.
b		My brother always cooks a surprise meal for us then.
c		Best, Jenny
d		Would you like to come and try this week's surprise?
e		Are you free on Friday night?
f		It's pear and bean omelette.
g		Please say you can come.
h		And for dessert it's some ice cream and strawberries.
i	1	Dear Jimmy,
j		Doesn't that sound good?

2 **Write out the email in your notebooks.**

3 **Write a paragraph describing your favourite or least favourite meal.**

Thirteenandsosmart.com

MY BLOG ABOUT MY DAY AND
OTHER IMPORTANT THINGS

FRIDAY, 17TH MARCH

Not a good day. My older brother Jeremy is cooking tonight. 'What's the problem?' I can hear you saying. Well, the problem is that you don't know my brother. You don't know how he cooks. And you don't know that every Friday is a nightmare for me because my parents go to their dance class. When they come back we all sit down and Jeremy starts serving what he calls 'another surprise meal'. Jeremy isn't a bad cook. He's a catastrophe!

First of all he always cooks too many things, like fish, steak, boiled ham, roast chicken and sausages. All on one plate! That's too much food for a week! How can one person eat all that in one meal? Mum and Dad don't say a word, of course. They're too polite. And they don't want to give up their dance classes.

Spaghetti tonight. When Jeremy says 'spaghetti' he doesn't say it. He sings it (he loves cooking spaghetti, well, he loves cooking anything!). But that doesn't make a difference. It tastes terrible. There isn't enough tomato sauce on it. There's too much pasta. And there's too much salt. Yuck! Another one of my brother's favourites is vegetable soup. It's always too spicy, and there are never enough vegetables in it. And he puts in little pieces of fish, steak, ham, chicken and sausages. You can guess where they're from. It's the left-overs from the week before.

My brother's desserts aren't bad. He gets them at the supermarket. It's usually ice cream with strawberries or chocolate mousse with mango. But, of course, there are never enough strawberries and there's never enough ice cream. I want to talk to Mum and Dad today. I want them to give up dancing. It's not healthy. You know what I mean. It's unhealthy for me when they go dancing every Friday …

GRAMMAR
too many / too much / (not) enough + noun

1 Complete the sentences with *much*, *many* and *enough* and then complete the rule.

1 He always cooks **too** _____ **things**.
2 There's **too** _____ **salt** in the spaghetti.
3 There's not _____ **tomato sauce** on it.
4 There aren't _____ **vegetables** in the soup.
5 There's not _____ **sugar** in my coffee.

> **RULE:** Use *too* [1]_____ with countable nouns, and *too* [2]_____ with uncountable nouns.
> Use *(not) enough* with [3]_____ and [4]_____ .

2 Complete with *too much*, *too many*, *not enough*.

1 There are _____ mushrooms on this pizza. I hate them.
2 There's _____ salt in this soup. I can't eat it.
3 There is _____ sugar in my coffee. Can I have some more, please?
4 There are _____ chairs. Can you stand?
5 There are _____ cars on the road. It's dangerous to ride my bike.
6 We've got _____ homework tonight. I want to watch TV.

too + adjective, (not +) adjective + enough

3 Use the example sentences to ⊙circle the correct options in the rule.

*His vegetable soup is always **too spicy**.*
*This pizza is **not hot enough**.*

> **RULE:**
> ● We use *too* + adjective to say that something is [1]*more / less* than we like or want.
> ● We use *not* + adjective + *enough* to say that something is [2]*more / less* than we like or want.

4 Complete the sentences.

0 The test is too easy. It's <u>*not hard enough.*</u>
1 The film isn't exciting enough. It's _____
2 The T-shirt is too expensive. It's _____
3 It's not warm enough today. It's _____
4 Your bike's too small for me. It's _____
5 His car's not fast enough. It's _____

5 Complete with *not enough* or *too*.

My dad always says there's [1]_____ much rain in the UK in the summer, and that it's [2]_____ hot _____ . He's right. And I feel that it's [3]_____ boring to spend holidays here. So I'm happy that we usually go to the south of Italy for our holidays. There are kilometres of beaches, and so there are never [4]_____ many tourists. I love the food there, that's why I often eat [5]_____ much.

Workbook page 29 ➤

VOCABULARY
Adjectives to talk about food

1 Write the adjectives under the photos.

roast | boiled | grilled | fried

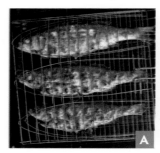 

A _____ B _____

C _____ D _____

2 Put the words in the list in order from 'very good' to 'very bad'.

nice | horrible | delicious | (a bit) boring

3 SPEAKING **Work in pairs. Ask and answer questions. Use the words from Exercise 2.**

boiled or roast beef? | grilled or fried chicken?
boiled or roast potatoes? | boiled or fried eggs?
grilled or fried fish?

> *What do you prefer, boiled or roast beef?*

> *Roast beef. It's delicious.*

4 How do you say these words in your language? Write two types of food next to each word.

sweet | spicy | savoury | fresh | tasty
yummy | fatty | disgusting | salty

sweet: chocolate, strawberries

Workbook page 30 ➤

The picnic

1 🔊 1.38 **Look at the photos and discuss the questions. Then listen and read and check your answers.**

What food and drink have Megan and Luke got?

Why is Olivia unhappy?

MEGAN A picnic. I love picnics. What a great idea, Ryan.

OLIVIA Yes, Ryan. It was an awesome idea.

RYAN Don't be so surprised. It's not my first one.

LUKE Umm. Actually, I think it probably is.

OLIVIA What drinks have you got, Megan?

MEGAN Let me see. I've got orange juice, lemonade and apple juice. Oh, and some water as well.

OLIVIA That's great. What about you, Ryan?

RYAN I've got fruit: apples and bananas. Oh, and a couple of chocolate bars.

OLIVIA Luke? What about the sandwiches?

LUKE Well, I've got ham. I've got chicken, and tuna, and I've got a steak sandwich too.

OLIVIA That's all? But what about me? I can't eat that.

LUKE Why not?

OLIVIA Because I've got a problem with eating meat. I'm a vegetarian, remember?

LUKE So what? You can have the tuna sandwich, then.

RYAN Oh, Luke! Olivia is really upset now.

LUKE Is she upset with me? Why? Tell me. I've got no idea.

MEGAN She's a vegetarian, Luke. She doesn't eat meat. It's important to her.

LUKE Don't vegetarians eat fish?

MEGAN Maybe some do, but not Olivia.

LUKE Oh no!

DEVELOPING SPEAKING

2 Work in pairs. Discuss what happens next in the story. Write down your ideas.

We think Olivia eats a chicken sandwich.

3 ▶ **EP2** Watch to find out how the story continues.

4 Mark the sentences T (True) or F (False).

1 Luke feels bad for not thinking about Olivia. ☐
2 Ryan has got lots of biscuits. ☐
3 Megan and Ryan play football against the other two. ☐
4 Luke secretly makes a phone call. ☐
5 They don't enjoy the football match. ☐
6 The pizza man brings Olivia a pizza with no meat on it. ☐

PHRASES FOR FLUENCY

1 Find the expressions 1–5 in the story. Who says them? Match them to the definitions a–f.

0 Actually, … _____Luke_____ | e |
1 … as well. _____ | ☐ |
2 … a couple of … _____ | ☐ |
3 What about (me)? _____ | ☐ |
4 So what? _____ | ☐ |
5 upset with … _____ | ☐ |

a too
b unhappy with
c one or two (but not many)
d What is the situation (for me)?
e In fact, …
f Why is that a problem?

2 Complete the conversations. Use the expressions in Exercise 1.

1 A Mum? John's got his sandwiches. But _____ me?
  B Well, I'm making _____ cheese and tomato sandwiches for you right now.
  A Cool! Can I have an apple _____ ?

2 A I broke your watch. I'm sorry. Are you _____ me?
  B Don't worry about it. _____ , it wasn't a very good watch.

3 A I can't go to the cinema. I've got homework.
  B _____ ? You can do it at the weekend.

WordWise

Expressions with *have got*

1 Complete the things that Luke and Olivia say.

1 I've got a _____ with eating meat.
2 I've got _____ idea.
3 You go on. I've got _____ to do first.

2 Complete with the expressions in the list.

a problem | an idea | a headache | time | something to do

0 A Dad! I've got *a problem* with my English homework.
  B English? Sorry! I can't help you.

1 A Are you OK? Is something wrong?
  B I've got _____ . I want to go to bed.

2 A What can we do this afternoon?
  B I don't know.
  C Oh, I've got _____ !

3 A Jan, can you help me, please?
  B I'm really sorry, Tom. The lesson starts in two minutes! I haven't got _____ .

4 A Let's go to town tomorrow.
  B Tomorrow? Sorry, no, I've got _____ tomorrow. It's a secret!

> Workbook page 30

FUNCTIONS

Apologising

1 Who says these sentences? Mark them O (Olivia) or L (Luke).

1 I'm really sorry. ___
2 I feel bad. ___
3 Don't worry. ___
4 It's OK. ___

2 🔊 **1.39** Complete the conversation. Listen and check. Then act it out in pairs.

MAN Oh no. I'm really [1] _____ .
WOMAN [2] _____ worry. It's not my favourite picture.
MAN But it's broken. I [3] _____ really bad.
WOMAN [4] _____ OK. Really. I don't really like it anyway.

3 Work in pairs. Write a short dialogue for the picture below. Act it out.

4 FAMILY TIES

OBJECTIVES

FUNCTIONS: asking for permission; talking about families
GRAMMAR: possessive adjectives and pronouns; *whose* and possessive *'s*; *was / were*
VOCABULARY: family members; feelings

READING

1 Find the pairs of words.

**daughter   brother   father
wife   husband   mother
son   sister**

2 SPEAKING Describe each person in the picture. Use two words from Exercise 1.

The girl is a daughter and a sister.

3 Work in pairs. Write down as many examples as you can of the following.

1 a TV brother and sister
2 a TV husband and wife

4 SPEAKING Compare your ideas with another pair.

5 ◁))1.40 Read and listen to the article on page 39. Do they mention any of the families you talked about?

6 Read the article again. Correct the information in these sentences.

1 Bart Simpson has got a cat called Santa's Little Helper.
2 Lisa Simpson has got one aunt.
3 Ben Tennyson is on holiday in Europe.
4 He can change into 12 different aliens.
5 Greg Heffley has got a little brother called Roderick.
6 His ideas are always successful.

TV Families

Who is your favourite TV family? We want to know. It's not easy. There are so many great families to choose from. But to help you start thinking, here are some of ours.

Everyone knows *The Simpsons*; Bart, his mum and dad Marge and Homer, his sisters Lisa and Maggie. And then there's Granddad and those horrible aunts, Patty and Selma. And let's not forget Bart's dog, Santa's Little Helper. I love watching this family and their adventures around the town of Springfield. They get into all kinds of trouble but they never forget they are a family. And they always make me laugh. I love this show. Thanks, Dad, for introducing it to me.

When I was eight, *Ben 10* was my favourite TV programme. The story is crazy. Ten-year-old Ben Tennyson is spending his summer holiday with his Grandpa and his cousin Gwen. They are driving around the USA. One day Ben finds a strange watch and puts it on. Suddenly he is an alien. With this watch he can turn into ten different space creatures. But he needs these powers because some other evil alien wants Ben's new watch. So Ben spends the rest of the holiday fighting lots of monsters from outer space. But, of course, he still has time to fight with his cousin too.

The Heffley family are the stars of *Diary of a Wimpy Kid*, a really popular series of books and films centred around Greg, the middle son of the family. Greg lives with his mum and dad, his little brother Manny and his big brother Roderick. He's just a 'normal' kid who writes about his life in a journal. OK, so the Heffley family are not really a 'TV' family but they show the films on TV a lot so we think we can choose them. We want the Heffleys on our list because they are so funny. And we really love Greg and all the problems he has with his great ideas that never work out.

So these are three of our favourite TV families. Now write in and tell us about yours.

■ THiNK VALUES ■

TV families

1 **Think about your favourite TV family. Tick (✓) the things they do.**

My favourite TV family is _____ .

- They help each other. ☐
- They fight a lot. ☐
- They laugh a lot. ☐
- They spend a lot of time together. ☐
- They talk about their problems. ☐
- They are good friends. ☐

2 **SPEAKING Work in pairs. Tell your partner about your favourite TV family. Are they a good family?**

> *The Simpsons are usually a good family because ...*

> *But sometimes they ...*

GRAMMAR
Possessive adjectives and pronouns

1 Complete the sentences with the words in the list. Look at the article on page 39 and check your answers.

our | ours | your | yours

1 Who are _____ favourite TV family?
2 Here are some of _____ .
3 These are three of _____ favourite TV families.
4 Now write in and tell us about _____ .

2 Complete the rule with *pronouns* and *adjectives*. Then complete the table.

> **RULE:** Possessive ^{1}_____ come before a noun to show who something belongs to: *It's my book.*
>
> Possessive ^{2}_____ can take the place of the possessive adjective and the noun: *The book is mine.*

possessive adjectives	possessive pronouns
0 It's __*my*__ book.	The book is __*mine*__
1 It's your book.	The book is _____ .
2 It's _____ book.	The book is hers.
3 It's _____ book.	The book is his.
4 It's our book.	The book is _____ .
5 It's _____ book.	The book is theirs.

whose and possessive *'s*

3 (Circle) the correct words and complete the rule.

A ^{1}*Whose / Who* son is Bart?
B Bart is ^{2}*Homer's / Homers'* son.
A ^{3}*Whose / Who's* Lisa's mum?
B Marge.

> **RULE:** To ask about possession, use the question word ^{1}_____ .
>
> To talk about possession, add ^{2}_____ to the end of a name / noun.
>
> If the name / noun ends in an -s, add the apostrophe (') after the -s.

4 (Circle) the correct words.

1 A *Whose / Who* phone is this?
  B Ask Jenny. I think it's *her / hers*.
2 Hey! That's *my / mine* sandwich not *your / yours*.
3 I'm sure that's *Kate's / Kates'* bike. It looks just like *her / hers*.
4 A *Whose / Who* do you sit next to in Maths?
  B *Rashid / Rashid's*.
5 A Is that your *parent's / parents'* dog?
  B Yes, I think it's *their / theirs*.

Workbook page 36

VOCABULARY
Family members

1 Read the text. Complete the spaces in the picture with the missing family words.

Here's a photo of my dad's side of the family. My dad's got a *big* brother called Bob. He's my *uncle* and he's great. He's so funny. His wife Jemma is my *aunt*, of course (and she's my dad's *sister-in-law*). She's also really nice. They've got two sons – Jimmy and his *little* brother Robin. They're my *cousins*. Jimmy is also my best friend.

Of course, my dad and Bob have the same mum and dad. They are my *grandparents*. I call them *Grandma Diana* and *Grandpa Roger*. They're really nice to me because I'm their only granddaughter.

2 **SPEAKING** Work in pairs. How many sentences can you make about the family in two minutes?

> Diana is Roger's wife.

> Jimmy is Jemma's son.

Workbook page 38

my dad ^{0} _Grandpa_ Roger ^{1}_____ Diana

Dad's ^{2}_____ brother
My ^{3}_____ Bob

My ^{4}_____
Jemma

Jimmy's ^{5}_____ brother
Robin (my ^{6}_____)

My ^{7}_____
Jimmy

LISTENING

1 **Read and match three of the sentences with the pictures. Write the numbers in the boxes.**

WHY MY FAMILY DRIVE ME MAD

1 My sister always wants to borrow my clothes. It drives me mad. (Lucy, 17)

2 My uncle tells really bad jokes. No one ever laughs – just him. (Howard, 15)

3 My dad never gives me any money. He's so mean. (Suzie, 16)

4 My grandpa just talks about the 'good-old days'. I'm not really interested. (Viv, 12)

5 I often fight with my parents about going out. They always want me to stay at home. (Tom, 14)

6 My brother plays games all day. He never lets me play. (Paul, 14)

2 ◀)) **1.41** **Listen to the conversations. What is the relationship between the speakers?**

Conversation 1: _____

Conversation 2: _____

3 ◀)) **1.41** **Listen again and answer the questions.**

1 What does Lucy's sister Kathy want to borrow?

2 Why does she want to borrow it?

3 Does Lucy say yes or no?

4 Where does Tom want to go?

5 What does his mum say?

6 What does his dad say?

Pronunciation

-er /ə/ at the end of words
Go to page 120. ◀))

FUNCTIONS
Asking for permission

1 **Complete the sentences from the listening.**

Asking for permission	Saying yes	Saying no
1 _____ I borrow your yellow and black shirt? 2 _____ I go out tonight?	Of course you can.	No, you 3 _____ .

2 **Write a short conversation for the picture.**

3 **Think of requests that you make to different members of your family. Write them down.**

Can I borrow ... ?   *Can I have ... ?*

Can I go ... ?   *Can I play ... ?*

4 **Read them to your partner. Can he/she guess who you say this to?**

READING

1 Look at the photos. How do you think these girls were heroes? Read the article and find out.

THE SWIMMING POOL HEROES

Miya Peyregne, aged nine, and her six-year-old sister Tiffany were in the swimming pool in the back garden of their house in Grandville, Michigan, USA. Their father David was with them. It was a lovely day. There wasn't a cloud in the sky.

Suddenly David shouted. He was in trouble. It was his legs. His legs weren't right. He was in pain.

Then he was under the water. The girls weren't scared but they were worried. Was it just a joke or was he really in trouble? Twenty seconds later he was still under the water. Now Miya was scared.

There was no time to wait. In seconds Miya was under the water with her father. He was heavy but with the help of the water she was able to pull him to one side of the pool. Now his head was out of the water. He was alive but he wasn't conscious.

There was a mobile phone in the house. Tiffany called the emergency services. Ten minutes later an ambulance was there. Soon their father was conscious again. The girls were relieved.

David still doesn't know what was wrong with his legs on that day. But he knows that his daughters were heroes and thanks them every day for saving his life. He is a very proud father.

2 Read the article again. Put the sentences in the correct order. There is one thing not mentioned in the article. Where do you think it goes?

a Miya goes under the water to help her dad. ☐
b Tiffany phones for an ambulance. ☐
c Their mother arrives home. ☐
d David has a problem with his legs. ☐
e David disappears under the water. ☐
f Miya and Tiffany are swimming with their dad, David. ☐

■ TRAIN TO THiNK ■

Making inferences

1 Work in pairs. Who says these sentences? Mark them M (Miya), T (Tiffany) or D (Dad).

1 'Help. I'm in trouble.' ☐
2 'What's wrong, Dad?' ☐
3 'Help him. Go under the water.' ☐
4 'Call an ambulance.' ☐
5 'My dad needs help.' ☐
6 'My heroes.' ☐

2 Work in pairs. Write one more thing to say to each person.

1 Miya   4 The ambulance driver
2 Tiffany   5 The girls' mother
3 David

3 **SPEAKING** Read your sentences to another pair for them to guess.

I think Miya says that.

That's probably Tiffany.

GRAMMAR
was / were

1 Look at the examples from the article on page 42. Circle the correct words.

1 It *was / were* a lovely day. There *wasn't / weren't* a cloud in the sky.

2 The girls *were / weren't* scared but they *were / weren't* worried.

3 *Was / Were* he really in trouble?

2 Complete the table.

Positive	Negative
I/he/she/it [0] __was__	I/he/she/it [1] _____ (was not)
You/we/they [0] __were__	You/we/they [2] _____ (were not)

Questions	Short answers
[3] _____ I/he/she/it?	Yes, I/he/she/it [4] _____ . No, I/he/she/it [5] _____ .
[6] _____ you/we/they?	Yes, you/we/they [7] _____ . No, you/we/they [8] _____ .

3 Complete the questions and answers with *was, were, wasn't* or *weren't*.

1 A _____ you in bed at 9 pm last night?
  B No, I _____ . I _____ in the kitchen with my mum and dad.

2 A _____ your teacher happy with your homework?
  B Yes she _____ . She _____ very happy with it.

3 A _____ it hot yesterday?
  B No, it _____ . It _____ really cold.

4 A _____ we at school yesterday?
  B No, we _____ . It _____ Sunday!

5 A _____ your parents born in the UK?
  B No, they _____ . They _____ born in India.

4 **SPEAKING** Work in pairs. Ask and answer the questions in Exercise 3.

Workbook page 37

VOCABULARY
Feelings

1 Match the sentences.

1 Our daughter was first in the race. ☐
2 It was 9 pm and Mum wasn't home. ☐
3 That wasn't a nice thing to say to Miriam. ☐
4 That maths lesson was really difficult. ☐
5 I wasn't expecting a big party. ☐
6 The students were really noisy. ☐
7 It was a really good horror film. ☐
8 The test was really hard. ☐

a She's really **upset** now.
b And the teacher was **angry**.
c I was very **surprised** to see so many people there.
d I'm really **confused** now.
e We are so **proud** of her.
f I was **relieved** when it was over.
g I was a bit **worried**. Where was she?
h I was really **scared** at the end of it.

2 Match the sentences in Exercise 1 with the pictures. Write the numbers 1–8.

Workbook page 38

A ☐

B ☐

C ☐

D ☐

E ☐

F ☐

G ☐

H ☐

Culture

1 Look at the photos. What can you see? What's the same in the two photos?

2 🔊 1.44 Read and listen to the article. Which countries do the photos show?

3 Do people celebrate Children's Day in your country? If so how do they celebrate it?

Around the world on Children's Day

In 1954 there was the first Universal Children's Day on 20th November to <u>celebrate</u> and protect children all over the world. This was <u>International</u> Children's Day but now many countries around the world have their own day each year when they celebrate their children.

1st June

BULGARIA: Parents do special things with their children and give them big **presents**. The day is like a second birthday for the children.

CHINA: This is a very special day in schools. They take the children on camping trips or trips to the cinema. Many children also get presents from their parents.

23rd April

TURKEY: This day is a **national** holiday in Turkey. On this day, Turkey invites groups of children from other countries to stay with Turkish families and celebrate with them.

24th July

VANUATU: Children spend the morning at school where they celebrate and have fun. At midday, the children are free to go home and spend the rest of the day with their parents. Some parents buy their children a present but the most important thing is for children and parents to have some time to spend **together**.

30th April

MEXICO: Children's day is called *El Día Del Niño*. Some schools close for the day, other schools have a special day for the children when they play games. The children also bring in their favourite food to **share** with their friends.

5th May

JAPAN: The official children's day, called *kodomo no hi*, is on 5th May. But some people in Japan celebrate two children's days. One on 3rd March for girls and one on 5th May for boys. On 5th May they fly carp streamers (a type of wind sock in the shape of a fish).

14th November

INDIA: Indians chose this day to celebrate because it is the birthday of the country's first Prime Minister, Jawaharlal Nehru. Nehru was famous for his love of children. On this day, the children organise the celebrations at their school. Their teachers sing and dance for the students.

4 **Read the article again. Answer the questions. Sometimes there is more than one correct answer.**

In which country …

1 do the children spend more time with their mum and dad?
2 do they have more than one Children's Day?
3 is Children's Day also a famous person's birthday?
4 do children get presents?
5 do children celebrate with children from other countries?
6 do children celebrate Children's Day at school?

5 SPEAKING **Work in small groups. Talk about the perfect Children's Day.**

> All children get a big present.
> School is closed for the whole day.
> Mum and Dad do your homework.

6 VOCABULARY **There are six words in bold/underlined in the article. Match the words with these meanings. Write the words.**

0 to have fun, do something special, for example on a friend's birthday — *celebrate*
1 with other people — _____
2 to do with a whole country — _____
3 to have something at the same time with other people — _____
4 to do with two or more countries — _____
5 something you give to a person on a special day — _____

WRITING
An invitation

1 **Read the emails. Answer the questions.**

1 Who is Dana?
2 Can Liam go to the party?

To: TinaB@thinkmail.com
Subject: Re: Party!

Hi Tina,

I'd love to come to your party on Friday but I've got a small problem. I've got football training from 6 to 7.30 pm. Can I arrive a bit late? Is that OK?

No problem with the playlist. I've got some great new songs.

See you Friday.

Liam

To: Liam_Walker@hooray.co.uk
Subject: Party!

Hi Liam,

Would you like to come to my house next Friday for a party at 7 pm? It's my cousin Dana's birthday.

My address is 32 Lime Street. Make a playlist please, I love your music.

Hope you can come. Let me know soon.

Tina

PS Don't tell Dana. It's a surprise.

---

2 **Match the sentences with the same meaning. Write a–e in the boxes.**

1 Would you like to come to my party? ☐
2 I'd love to come to your party. ☐
3 I'm sorry I can't come to your party. ☐
4 Make a playlist, please. ☐
5 Don't tell Dana. ☐

a I don't want Dana to know.
b Can you make a playlist?
c Can you come to my party?
d I'd love to come but I can't.
e I'd be very happy to accept your invitation.

3 **Which pairs of sentences in Exercise 2 can you use to do these things?**

1 give an order _____
2 accept an invitation _____
3 make a request _____
4 make an invitation _____
5 refuse an invitation _____

4 **Read the invitation again. Answer the questions.**

1 What is the invitation for?
2 What special requests does Tina make?

5 **You want to invite a friend to your house. What information should you include? Tick (✓) the correct answers.**

1 Your address. ☐
2 How many brothers and sisters you've got. ☐
3 The time you want them to come. ☐
4 The reason. ☐
5 Who your favourite singer is. ☐
6 The day or date you want them to come. ☐

6 **Write an invitation (50 words). Choose one of these reasons. Include a special request or instruction.**

- It's your birthday.
- You've got a great new DVD to watch.
- You've got a new computer game.

CAMBRIDGE ENGLISH: Key

■ THiNK EXAMS ■

READING AND WRITING
Part 2: Multiple-choice sentence completion   Workbook page 61

1 Read the sentences about a trip to a café. Choose the best word (A, B or C) for each space.

0	99% in my maths test! Mum is really _____ .		(A) proud	B scared	C upset
1	She takes me and my little _____ to the café for an ice cream.		A uncle	B aunt	C sister
2	I eat _____ of ice cream.		A many	B any	C a lot
3	My mum doesn't want her ice cream, so I eat _____ too.		A her	B mine	C hers
4	And then I drink _____ cola.		A not enough	B too many	C too much
5	I _____ feel very well, so we go home.		A not	B don't	C am not

Part 3: Dialogue matching   Workbook page 35

2 Complete the conversation. What does Anita say to the waiter?

For questions 1–5, choose the correct letter A–H.

WAITER   Can I help you?

ANITA   (0) __G__

WAITER   Of course, here you are.

(5 minutes later)

WAITER   OK, so what can I get you?

ANITA   (1) _____

WAITER   Of course. Would you like a starter?

ANITA   (2) _____

WAITER   And what would you like to drink?

ANITA   (3) _____

WAITER   And would you like a dessert?

ANITA   (4) _____

WAITER   OK, so that's a cheese omelette and strawberry ice cream.

(20 minutes later)

ANITA   (5) _____

WAITER   Of course. I'll be back soon.

A   How much is it?

B   An orange juice, please.

C   I'd like a cheese omelette, please.

D   And the orange juice.

E   Can I have the bill?

F   No, thanks. Just the omelette.

G   ~~I'd like to see the menu, please.~~

H   Yes, please. Can I have some strawberry ice cream?

LISTENING
Part 3: Three-option multiple-choice   Workbook page 43

3 ◀))1.45 Listen to Jackie talking to Oliver about her family. For each question, choose the right answer (A, B or C).

0	The party was last	(A) Friday evening.	B Saturday evening.	C Friday afternoon.
1	The party was for Oliver's	A brother.	B dad.	C uncle.
2	Oliver's uncle is	A 20.	B 34.	C 44.
3	Oliver's aunt is called	A Anna.	B Carla.	C Ruth.
4	Mike is Oliver's	A brother.	B dad.	C cousin.
5	Oliver has got	A two sisters.	B one sister.	C one sister and one brother.

VOCABULARY

1 Complete the sentences with the words in the list. There are two extra words.

angry | big | boiled | grilled | relieved | scared
grandparents | carrots | confused | spicy | chicken | proud

1 I don't like many vegetables – just peppers and _____ .
2 I was really worried about the exam so I was _____ when it was over.
3 The curry is too _____ . I can't eat it.
4 It was a really stupid thing to do. My parents were really _____ with me.
5 To make _____ potatoes you need to cook them in water for about 20 minutes.
6 There was a strange noise outside the house. We were a bit _____ .
7 Nigel's a vegetarian. He doesn't eat _____ .
8 I don't really understand this homework. I'm a bit _____ .
9 Freddie's my _____ brother. I'm 14 and he's 20.
10 My mum's mother and father are my _____ .

/10

GRAMMAR

2 Complete the sentences with the words in the list.

much | many | ours | our | was | were

1 How _____ sugar do you want in your coffee?
2 It _____ really cold yesterday.
3 That's not your dog, it's _____ .
4 There are too _____ socks on your bedroom floor!
5 _____ dog's called Spike.
6 Where _____ you last night?

3 Find and correct the mistake in each sentence.

1 This salad has got too much beans.
2 That's not your sandwich. It's my.
3 My parents was very proud of my school report.
4 I like Clara and I really like hers sister too.
5 How many water do you want?
6 I think this is Kevins' book.

/12

FUNCTIONAL LANGUAGE

4 Write the missing words.

1 A I'm late. I'm really _____ .
   B Don't _____ . We've still got lots of time.
2 A I _____ this question is really difficult.
   B I think _____ too.
3 A _____ I borrow your bike, Dad?
   B Of _____ you can.
4 A Can I go _____ tonight?
   B No, you _____ .

/8

MY SCORE [   ] /30

| 22 – 30 |
| 10 – 21 |
| 0 – 9 |

47

5 IT FEELS LIKE HOME

A

B

C

D

E

F

READING

1 ◀)) **1.46** Match the words in the list with the photos. Write 1–6 in the boxes. Then listen, check and repeat.

1 kitchen | 2 bedroom | 3 bathroom
4 living room | 5 dining room | 6 garden

2 Match the verbs in the list with the rooms in Exercise 1. (Some verbs go with more than one room.)

eat | sleep | cook | wash
watch TV | play football

3 **SPEAKING** Work in pairs. Have you got the same ideas? What other activities do you do in these rooms?

I talk to my dad in the kitchen.

I sing in the bathroom.

4 **SPEAKING** Look at the photos on page 49. What can you say about the house?

5 ◀)) **1.47** Read and listen to the magazine article. ✳ Choose the correct option A, B or C.

1 The queue of people wanted to help James May to buy a house.
   A Right   B Wrong   C Doesn't say

2 They finished building the house in one month.
   A Right   B Wrong   C Doesn't say

3 The LEGO fridge worked.
   A Right   B Wrong   C Doesn't say

4 James May liked the bed.
   A Right   B Wrong   C Doesn't say

5 There were photos of the house on a Facebook page.
   A Right   B Wrong   C Doesn't say

6 A charity for children has got the pieces of LEGO now.
   A Right   B Wrong   C Doesn't say

The LEGO® House

A few years ago in August, there was a very long queue of people in the countryside near London, in England. Some people started queuing at 4.30 in the morning. Why were they there? They wanted to help James May, a TV presenter, to build a house. But this was not an ordinary house. No, this was a LEGO house.

Together, 1,200 people used 3.3 million (yes, 3,300,000) LEGO toy bricks to make a real house.

It was part of a TV show called *Toy Stories*. In the programmes, James May used traditional toys to make 'real' things. Why LEGO? Well, because when he was young, James May loved LEGO and played with it all the time.

The people finished building the house on 17 September, almost seven weeks after they started. Everything was LEGO. All the walls, doors and windows were LEGO. There was a LEGO bedroom and a LEGO bed. There was a LEGO bathroom with a LEGO toilet and a shower – and they worked! In the kitchen there was a LEGO fridge (but no cooker) and there were LEGO tables and chairs. There was even a LEGO cat. James May stayed in the house one night and was surprised because the bed was quite comfortable.

At first, a theme park called LEGOLAND planned to buy the house, but later they decided not to. James May tried to find another buyer. He started a Facebook page and asked other people to buy it, but nobody wanted it. So on 22 September, they started to take the house to pieces. A few days later, there wasn't a LEGO house any more.

James May was not happy about it as more than 1,000 people worked hard to build the house and everything inside it. Other people were not so sad. The television company donated the three million LEGO pieces to a charity for children.

■ THiNK VALUES ■

Community spirit

1 Read what people said about the LEGO house. Match the activities a–d with the comments 1–4.

a working together   c having fun
b being creative   d caring for others

1 We really enjoyed this – we laughed a lot. ☐

2 The idea of building a LEGO cat was really interesting. ☐

3 I loved being with so many people, doing the same thing! ☐

4 I think it's great that they donated the LEGO pieces to a charity for children. ☐

2 SPEAKING Put the activities a–d in Exercise 1 in order of importance for you. Compare your ideas with a partner.

I think working together is really important. It's my number 1.

Me too. It's my number 2.

What's your number 1?

Caring for others.

GRAMMAR
Past simple (regular verbs)

1 Find the past simple forms of these verbs in the article and write them below. Then complete the rules.

0	start	*started*	5	stay	_____
1	want	_____	6	plan	_____
2	use	_____	7	decide	_____
3	finish	_____	8	try	_____
4	work	_____	9	ask	_____

> **RULE:** Use the past simple to talk about finished actions in the past.
>
> **With regular verbs:**
> * We usually add ¹_____ to the verb (e.g. *start – started* / *stay – stayed*).
> * If the verb ends in *-e* (e.g. *use*), we add ²_____ .
> * If a short verb ends in consonant + vowel + consonant (e.g. *plan*), we double the ³_____ and add *-ed*.
> * We add *-ed* to verbs ending in vowel + *-y* (e.g. *stayed*).
> * If the verb ends in consonant + *-y* (e.g. *try*), we change the *-y* to ⁴_____ and add ⁵_____ .

2 Complete the sentences. Use the past simple form of the verbs.

0 When my granddad was young, he _*played*_ (play) with LEGO all the time.

1 We _____ (start) to paint our house last month, and we _____ (finish) yesterday.

2 She _____ (decide) to change her bedroom, so she _____ (paint) the walls pink.

3 We _____ (try) to find another house last year because we _____ (want) to move.

4 I _____ (visit) my aunt and uncle because they _____ (want) to show me their new flat.

5 My parents _____ (study) lots of ideas for a new kitchen before they _____ (order) it.

6 On my last holiday, I _____ (stay) with my grandparents and _____ (help) them tidy up the garden.

7 Last weekend Jack _____ (plan) to organise his room but he _____ (watch) television instead.

Workbook page 46

> ## Pronunciation
> *-ed* endings /d/, /t/, /ɪd/
> **Go to page 120.**

VOCABULARY
Furniture

1 🔊 **1.50** Match the words with the photos. Write 1–12 in the boxes. Then listen, check and repeat.

1 armchair | 2 carpet | 3 cooker | 4 curtains
5 desk | 6 lamp | 7 mirror | 8 shelves
9 shower | 10 sofa | 11 toilet | 12 wardrobe

A   B
C   D
E   F
G   H
I   J
K   L

2 **SPEAKING** Work in pairs. Where are these things in your house? Tell your partner.

> *There are mirrors in our bathroom, in my parents' bedroom and in our living room.*

Workbook page 48

LISTENING

1 **SPEAKING** Work in pairs. Describe the pictures.

2 **◁)) 1.51** Listen to four people talking about 'home'. Write the names under the correct pictures.

Sophie | James | Mia | Daniel

3 **◁)) 1.51** Listen again. Complete the table with the missing information.

	What is home?	What I like doing there.
Sophie	Home is where I feel ¹_____ .	²_____
James	Somewhere ³_____ .	⁴_____
Mia	The ⁵_____ in our flat.	⁶_____
Daniel	With ⁷_____ in the garden.	⁸_____

GRAMMAR
Modifiers: *quite, very, really*

1 Write the name of the person from Exercise 3 who says these things. Then underline the words before the adjectives and complete the rule.

1 I feel really happy there.   _____
2 Our kitchen is quite small.   _____
3 The armchair is very comfortable.   _____

> **RULE:** Use words *very, really* and *quite* to say more about an adjective.
>
> The words *very* and ¹_____ are used to make an adjective stronger. The word ²_____ usually means 'a little bit'.

2 Write true sentences about your home using the words.

0 kitchen – big / small
   Our kitchen isn't very big / It's quite small.
1 bedroom – tidy / untidy
2 sofa – comfortable / uncomfortable
3 home – busy / quiet   **Workbook page 47** ▶

■ THiNK SELF-ESTEEM ■
Feeling safe

1 Think about the questions and make notes.

1 Where do you feel 'at home'? Describe the place.
2 What's most important for you there? (furniture? things? colours? people?)
3 What does that place feel like for you? (relaxing? safe? comfortable?)

2 **SPEAKING** Write 2 or 3 sentences about where you feel at home. Read them out in groups.

> I feel at home in my bedroom. My bed is quite small but it's very comfortable. I like lying on it and thinking about my life.

> I feel at home when I'm with my family. My mum and dad are great and my brother is my best friend. I love doing things with them.

> I feel at home in the living room. Our sofa is really comfortable. I love sitting there on my own reading a good book.

READING

1 Read Jenny's holiday blog and complete the sentences with a word or a number.

DAY 5

Dad gets it right! (finally)

Day five of the Italian adventure and we're in Naples. We arrived here early yesterday morning, but as usual we were only at the hotel for about five minutes before Dad wanted to take us somewhere. This time it was to the ancient city of Pompeii near Naples. I didn't really want to go. I wanted to go shopping for shoes.

We travelled there by train. The journey didn't take long – but long enough for Dad to tell us a bit about the history. Many years ago, Pompeii was a large Italian city near a volcano called Mount Vesuvius – then on 24 August 79 CE – the volcano erupted and completely covered the city in ash. It killed about 20,000 people. But the ash didn't destroy the buildings and now, 2,000 years later, you can walk around the city and see how people lived all those years ago.

2,000-year-old houses: thanks, Dad – really boring, I thought, but I was wrong! The houses were very interesting. Most of them were really big with lots of rooms (so lots of space to get away from annoying brothers and sisters!) There were paintings and mosaics all over the walls. I'd love a Roman mosaic of One Direction on my bedroom wall. Also, I was amazed at the bathrooms. I'd love a big bathroom in our house – ours is so small!

I got really interested in Pompeii. I wasn't bored at all. In fact, I've got lots of ideas for our house when we get home!

Mount Vesuvius – a real ¹_____ . (I hope it doesn't erupt!)

More than ²_____ people died here, all of them covered in ash.

The paintings and ³_____ are really beautiful.

The houses in this ancient city are more than ⁴_____ years old.

---

2 Answer the questions.

1 Where is Jenny's family staying at the moment?
2 How did they go to Pompeii?
3 What did Jenny's dad tell them about on the way there?
4 When did Vesuvius erupt?
5 What did Jenny like about the Pompeii houses?
6 What was Jenny's overall opinion of Pompeii?

WRITING

Use your answers in Exercise 2 to write a summary of the text in no more than 100 words.

Jenny didn't want to go to Pompeii and ...

GRAMMAR
Past simple negative

1 Compete the sentences from Jenny's blog and then complete the rule.

1 I _____ really want to go.
2 The journey _____ take long.
3 The ash _____ destroy the buildings.

> **RULE:** To make any verb negative in the past simple, use _____ + the base form of the verb.

2 Here are some more things Jenny wrote about Pompeii. Make them negative.

0 We visited all of the houses.
   We didn't visit all of the houses.
1 I wanted to go home.
2 The poor people lived in big houses.
3 Dad ordered a pizza for lunch.
4 It rained in the afternoon.

3 **SPEAKING** Work in pairs. Tell your partner two things that you did and two things that you didn't do last weekend. Choose from the verbs in the list.

work | climb | play | travel | clean
help | study | use | dance | walk

I didn't watch any TV.   *I visited my friends.*

Workbook page 47

VOCABULARY
adjectives with -ed / -ing

1 How is Jenny feeling? Write the adjectives under the pictures.

annoyed | relaxed | bored | interested | amazed

1 _____   2 _____

> **LOOK!** We use -ed adjectives to say how we feel about something.
>
> We use -ing adjectives to say what we think about something or to describe something.

2 What did Jenny say about Pompeii? Complete the sentences with *interested* or *interesting*.

1 I got really _____ in Pompeii.
2 The houses were very _____ .

3 (Circle) the correct words.

1 I get *annoyed / annoying* when people ignore me.
2 His painting was brilliant. I was *amazed / amazing*.
3 Bob talks about football all the time! He's really *bored / boring*.
4 A hot shower is always very *relaxed / relaxing*.
5 I think Maths is really *interested / interesting*.

4 Complete the sentences so that they are true for you.

1 I'm never bored when _____ .
2 I find _____ really annoying.
3 _____ is the most amazing singer.
4 I'm really interested in _____ .
5 I'm never relaxed when _____ .

5 **SPEAKING** Work in pairs. Compare your answers.

Workbook page 48

WRITING
A blog post

1 Think about a real holiday that you went on or an invented holiday. Make notes about these questions.

1 Where did you go?
2 Who did you go with?
3 What did you do that was very special / different?
4 What did you like / not like about the holiday?
5 What was *boring / exciting / amazing / interesting / annoying* about the holiday?

2 Use your notes from Exercise 1 to write a blog post about your holiday. Write about 120–150 words. Write three paragraphs.

Paragraph 1 – your answers to 1 and 2
Paragraph 2 – your answer to 3
Paragraph 3 – your answers to 4 and 5

3 _____   4 _____

5 _____

Hey, look at that guy!

1 Look at the photos and answer the questions.

What do you think the four friends are saying about the man? What do they know about him?

2 ◀》1.52 Now read and listen to the photostory. Check your answers.

RYAN Stop looking at your satnav – we know how to get to school.
OLIVIA Very funny. Hey, look at that guy!
RYAN What about him?
MEGAN I think he was here yesterday too.

LUKE So? A homeless guy. It's not a big deal.
RYAN That's right.
OLIVIA He's got problems. Don't you care?
RYAN Well, to be honest – no, not very much.

MEGAN But it's really sad!
OLIVIA I know what you mean. I watched a programme on TV a while ago about homeless people. Awful!
MEGAN Can you imagine? No place to live. It must be horrible.
LUKE Well, I'm sure that's true. But it's not really our problem.

OLIVIA Let's go and talk to him.
RYAN Hang on! Do you think that's a good idea?
MEGAN What do you mean? He's poor, but that doesn't mean he's dangerous.
LUKE OK, maybe not dangerous. He's probably not very nice, though.
OLIVIA Maybe he needs help.

DEVELOPING SPEAKING

3 Work in pairs. Discuss what happens next in the story. Write down your ideas.

We think the boys go to school but Megan and Olivia talk to the man.

4 ▶️ EP3 Watch to find out how the story continues.

5 Put the sentences in the correct order. Write 1–8 in the boxes.

- [ ] **a** The students decide to ask somebody from a charity for help.
- [ ] **b** The girls are worried about the man.
- [ ] **c** When they go back to the park, the man gives Olivia her necklace.
- [1] **d** The friends are on their way to school.
- [ ] **e** Other students start laughing at her.
- [ ] **f** Ryan tells the other students about the homeless person.
- [ ] **g** In the park, they see a homeless person.
- [ ] **h** The teacher notices that Olivia is not paying attention.

PHRASES FOR FLUENCY

1 Find these expressions in the story. Who says them?

1 … not a big deal. _____
2 …, to be honest, … _____
3 I know what you mean. _____
4 it's not really our problem. _____
5 Hang on! _____
6 …, though. _____

2 Use the expressions in Exercise 1 to complete the dialogues.

1 **A** She's usually a nice girl. She sometimes gets a bit angry, _____ .
   B _____ . Yesterday she really shouted at me!

2 **A** I need help. You've got to help me with my homework!
   B _____ ! It's *your* homework – so really, _____ .

3 **A** It's only a small test tomorrow. Ten questions. It's _____ . Right?
   B Well, _____ , I'm a bit worried about it.

WordWise
Phrasal verbs with *look*

1 Look at these sentences from the story. Complete them with the words from the list.

after | up | for | at | into

1 Hey, look _____ that guy!
2 The charity looks _____ homeless people.
3 I'm just looking it _____ on my phone.
4 We need to look _____ why he's homeless.
5 Let's look _____ him.

2 (Circle) the correct word in each dialogue.

1 **A** What's Janet doing?
   B She's looking *after / like* the baby.
2 **A** Why are you looking *for / at* me like that?
   B Because I'm angry with you.
3 **A** I can't find my pen.
   B I'll help you look *after / for* it.
4 **A** Do the police know what happened?
   B No, they are still looking *for / into* it.
5 **A** What does this word mean?
   B I don't know. Let's look it *after / up* in the dictionary.

▶ Workbook page 48

FUNCTIONS
Making suggestions

1 Complete the sentences from the story with words from the lists. Then write ✓ (agree), ✗ (disagree) or ? (uncertain).

A ~~How~~ | could | Let's | Why
B ~~idea~~ | do | great | sure

0 **A** ___*How*___ about asking our parents for money?
   B I don't think that's a good ___*idea*___ . ✗

1 **A** _____ don't we try and help him?
   B I'm not so _____ .

2 **A** _____ give him our school lunch.
   B Let's _____ that.

3 **A** We _____ take him a bit of food after school.
   B I think that's a _____ idea.

ROLE PLAY At a market

2 Work in pairs. Student A: Go to page 127. Student B: Go to page 128. Take two or three minutes to prepare. Then have a conversation.

6 BEST FRIENDS

OBJECTIVES

FUNCTIONS: talking about past events; saying what you like doing alone and with others; talking about friends and friendships

GRAMMAR: past simple (irregular verbs); double genitive; past simple questions

VOCABULARY: past time expressions; personality adjectives

READING

1  **Look at the photos. Say what the people are doing.**

> They're surfing the Internet.

2 **SPEAKING** **Match these words with the photos and compare with a partner. (Some words go with more than one photo.)**

alone | together | happy
sad | bored | excited

> In photo 1 they're together and they're excited.

3 **SPEAKING** **Work in pairs. Talk about things you like doing alone and other things you like doing together with other people. Here are some ideas to help you.**

watch a film | walk
do homework | study | read
have breakfast | go shopping

> I like going shopping with friends. I don't like going alone! I like doing homework alone.

4 Look at the photos on page 57. What kind of television show is this? Who are the boy and the girl?

5 **◁))1.53** Read and listen to the web article. Check your ideas.

6 Read the article again. Correct the information in these sentences.

1 Their parents had the idea of them singing together.
2 Jonathan thought that Charlotte didn't look right for the show.
3 Charlotte and Jonathan were the same age.
4 Everyone laughed when Charlotte and Jonathan came out.
5 Simon Cowell said that Jonathan needed to sing with another girl.
6 Jonathan told Simon Cowell that he wanted to go home.
7 Jonathan and Charlotte came first in the competition.
8 They recorded a song called *Together*.

Together ☆

In a school in England, a few years ago, a teenage girl heard a boy singing in another room. She liked it, and found out that the boy's name was Jonathan Antoine. The girl – Charlotte Jaconelli – also liked singing. A little later, the music teacher at school suggested that they could sing together. They did, and they started singing together as a duo. They also became very good friends. They even sang together at the music teacher's wedding.

Around that time, there was a television programme called *Britain's Got Talent* – a show to find new singers and performers. Charlotte wanted to enter the show with Jonathan but he was worried about the way he looked. However, Charlotte persuaded him and they went on the show. Charlotte was 16 and Jonathan was 17.

They did the first audition in April 2012. When they came onto the stage, they were very nervous. The four judges didn't think they looked good. Some people in the audience laughed when they saw them. Then they began to sing and everyone was amazed. They sang incredibly well – especially Jonathan. When they finished, people stood up and clapped.

All the judges thought Charlotte and Jonathan were great, but one judge, Simon Cowell, suggested that Jonathan sing on his own without Charlotte because, although she was good, he was fantastic.

Jonathan didn't think for long. He looked at his friend, and then looked back at the judges, and said that he wanted to stay in the competition with Charlotte. They carried on together, but they didn't win the competition – they came second. (A dancing dog won!) However, they weren't disappointed.

A few weeks later, Simon Cowell gave them the chance to record a CD. They made the CD, and then they thought about a title for it. They chose the word: 'Together'.

■ THiNK VALUES ■

Friendship and loyalty

1 **Choose the best way to finish this sentence.**

I think this story tells us that, in life, it is important …

1 … to look good.
2 … to be good at what you do.
3 … to come first.
4 … to look after your friends.
5 … to be nice to other people.
6 … to have lots and lots of friends.

2 **SPEAKING** Compare your ideas with a partner.

3 **SPEAKING** Choose three of the values in Exercise 1. Put them in order of importance for you (1, 2, 3). Then compare with others.

> I think the most important thing is to look after your friends.

> That's my number 3. I think it's really important to be nice to other people.

GRAMMAR
Past simple (irregular verbs)

1 **Read these sentences about the article on page 57. All the verbs are in the past simple. How are the verbs in 1 different from the verbs in 2?**

  1 She **liked** singing.
      They **started** as a duo.
      Some people **laughed**.

  2 They **sang** together.
      People **stood** up.
      We **came** here as a duo.

2 **Look back at the article on page 57. Write the past simple forms of these verbs.**

0	find	_found_	4	think	_____
1	become	_____	5	come	_____
2	go	_____	6	give	_____
3	see	_____	7	make	_____

3 **Find at least four more irregular past simple forms in the article on page 57. Write the verbs.**

4 **Correct these two sentences from the article. Make them negative.**

  1 Jonathan thought for a long time.
  2 They won the competition.

5 **Look at the pictures and the prompts and write the sentences in the past simple.**

Workbook page 54

VOCABULARY
Past time expressions

1 **Complete the lists with appropriate expressions.**

When we talk about the past, we often use expressions like these:

- yesterday, yesterday ¹_____ , yesterday afternoon
- last night, last week, last ²_____ , last December
- an hour ago, two weeks ago, a month ago, ³_____ ago

2 **Complete the sentences with a time expression with *ago*.**

  0 Andy is twenty. He left school when he was sixteen.
      Andy left school four years ago.

  1 It's 8 o'clock. I had breakfast at 7 o'clock.
      I had breakfast _____

  2 It's 10.20. The film began at 10.00.
      The film _____

  3 It's December. Your holiday was in July.
      My holiday _____

3 **Complete the sentences with your own information. Use irregular verbs.**

  1 A year ago, I _____ .
  2 Ten years ago, I _____ .
  3 Last year, I _____ .
  4 Yesterday morning, I _____ .
  5 Last night, I _____ .

Workbook page 56

1 We / go / to Italy but we / go / to Rome.
   We went to Italy but we didn't
   go to Rome.

2 I / see / Mark but I / see / Alicia.
   _____
   _____

3 Sue / come / to my party / but Dan / come.
   _____
   _____

4 I make / sandwiches but I / make / cake.
   _____
   _____

LISTENING

1 **Which sentences do you agree with?**

1 Footballers are never friends with players from other teams.

2 Footballers never help other players.

3 Footballers only want to win cups.

2 ◁)) **1.54** **Listen to a story about Cristiano Ronaldo. Tick (✓) the correct box.**

The two friends think the story is …

☐ certainly true.

☐ possibly true.

☐ certainly not true.

3 ◁)) **1.54** **Listen again and choose the right answer A, B or C.**

1 What was the family name of Ronaldo's friend?
   A Albert
   B The boy doesn't remember.
   C The boy didn't find the name.

2 How many places were there at the football school?
   A one   B two   C three

3 Why did Albert pass the ball to Cristiano?
   A Because Albert wanted a friend.
   B Because Albert was tired.
   C Because Cristiano was a better player.

4 What was the final score of the game?
   A 1–1   B 2–0   C 3–0

5 What is Albert's job now?
   A He's a footballer.
   B We don't know.
   C He drives cars.

6 What did Ronaldo give to his friend?
   A A car.
   B A house.
   C A car and a house.

4 **SPEAKING** **Work in pairs. Tell your partner about a great present someone gave you.**

> Last year my … gave me a … . I was really happy / excited because … .

GRAMMAR
Double genitive

1 **Read the sentence. Then choose the correct options to complete the rule.**

Ronaldo was there, and there was <u>a friend of his</u> called Albert.

> **RULE:** We form the 'double genitive' with noun + *of* + possessive ¹*pronoun / adjective* (*mine, yours, his, hers, ours, yours, theirs*).
>
> We also form the 'double genitive' with noun + *of* + possessive adjective (*my, your, his, her, our, your, their*) + noun + possessive *'s*.
>
> We use it to talk about ²*one of many things / many things that we have.*

2 **Circle the correct words.**

0 She's a friend of *me* / *mine*.

1 Mr Smith is a teacher of *my sister* / *my sister's*.

2 She's a cousin of *John* / *John's*.

3 Mrs Jones is a neighbour of *ours* / *us*.

3 **Rewrite the underlined parts of the sentences.**

0 See that man? He's <u>my father's friend</u>.
   He's _*a friend of my father's*_ .

1 Steve is <u>our friend</u>.
   Steve is _____ .

2 Mike borrowed <u>my shirt</u>.
   Mike borrowed _____ .

3 I lost <u>my mum's book</u>.
   I lost _____ .

> Workbook page 55

■ TRAIN TO THiNK ■

Making decisions

1 **Draw a mind map.**

● Complete the three circles with names of people who are close to you (friends, family).

● What do these people like? Write your ideas on the lines.

2 **SPEAKING** **Work in groups. Imagine it's their birthdays. Show your mind maps, make suggestions and decide on a present for each person.**

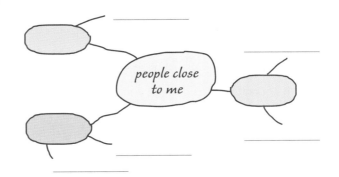

people close to me

READING

1 Read the magazine article quickly. Complete the sentences.

1 Richard and Sharon met for the first time on _____ .

2 The second time they met, they went _____ .

2 Read the article again. Put the events in the order they happened. Write the numbers 1–8.

☐	a	Richard and Sharon go to a show together.
☐	b	Richard has an accident.
☐	c	Richard gives Sharon a present.
☐	d	Sharon saves Richard's life.
☐	e	Richard goes to hospital.
☐	f	Sharon calls Richard.
1	g	Richard goes surfing.
☐	h	Richard sees Sharon for the first time.

3 **SPEAKING** Work in pairs. Tell the story. Use the ideas in Exercise 2. Put them into the past simple tense.

> *Richard went surfing. He had an accident ...*

FUNCTIONS
Talking about past events

1 Think about a time when you made a new friend. Make notes.

- Who?
- Where?
- When?
- What happened?

2 In pairs tell your story.

> *I met my friend Al five years ago. I was on holiday in France with my family. We were in a small hotel. Al's family were in the same hotel. We made friends on the first day and spent all the holiday together.*

Real life

How we met

This week lifeguard Sharon Evans and student Richard Lambert tell our reporter about their friendship and how they almost never met.

So first of all, when and where did you meet?

Richard We first met in 2012, one morning at about 10.30 am on Bondi Beach, in Sydney.

Sharon Actually, we met in the water.

OK, so how did you meet?

Richard I was out in the deep water on my surfboard when another board knocked me on the head. The next thing I knew, I was on the beach looking up at this face.

Sharon I was on the beach that day. I saw what happened so I swam out and brought Richard back in. He was unconscious, but luckily I got him to start breathing again. But for a minute I thought he was dead.

Richard And then they took me to hospital. I didn't have a chance to even say thanks to Sharon.

So what did you do?

Richard There was a really big show the next week with a popular Belgian-Australian singer called Gotye. I bought two tickets for Sharon and left them at work for her a few days later. I thought she could take someone with her. I also left her a note to say thanks with my telephone number on it.

Sharon He was really generous. They were expensive tickets.

Did you take a friend to the show?

Sharon I didn't know who to take and then I had a great idea.

What was it?

Richard Well, when I got home from work that day there was a voicemail on my phone. It was Sharon. She invited me to go with her. We had a great time. She was so cheerful and easy-going. We became really good friends right away.

GRAMMAR
Past simple questions

1 **Put the words in order to make questions. Check your answers in the article on page 60.**

1 do / did / what / you / ?   2 did / you / meet / how / ?   3 friend / show / take / you / a / to / did / the / ?

2 **Complete the table.**

Question	Answer
¹_____ I/you/he/she/we/they enjoy the show?	Yes, I/you/he/she/we/they ³_____ . No, I/you/he/she/we/they ⁴_____ (did not).
What time ²_____ I/you/he/she/we/they get home?	I/you/he/she/we/they ⁵_____ home at midnight.

3 **Match the questions and answers.**

1 Did you have a good weekend?
2 Did you play computer games yesterday?
3 Where did you meet your best friend?
4 Who did you text yesterday?
5 What did you have for dinner last night?

a Yes, I did. I completed four levels.
b We met at school four years ago.
c We had chicken and chips.
d No, I didn't. It rained all the time.
e I texted my best friend.

4 **SPEAKING** **Work in pairs. Ask the questions 1–5 and give your own answers.** Workbook page 55

VOCABULARY
Personality adjectives

Look at the pictures. Read the sentences and write the names under the people.

Thank you.

It's OK. Don't worry.

1 _____
2 _____
3 _____
4 _____
5 _____
6 _____
7 _____
8 _____

MY FRIENDS

- Nick is intelligent. He knows a lot about everything
- Amelia is cheerful. She's always got a smile on her face.
- Kai is jealous. He's not happy when you talk to other friends.
- Ben is helpful. He's always ready to help you.
- Ruby is confident. She's not scared to talk in public.
- Liz is generous. She's always happy to share her things with you.
- Chloe is easy-going. She never gets angry about anything.
- Connor is funny. He always makes me laugh.

Pronunciation
Stressed syllables in words
Go to page 120.

Workbook page 56

Culture

1 Look at the photos of friends. Who's having a good time? Who's having a bad time?

2 🔊 1.57 Read and listen to the web page. Five people commented on the different myths about friendship. Match the people to the myths.

Myth 1 _____ Myth 2 _____ Myth 3 _____ Myth 4 _____ Myth 5 _____

3 **SPEAKING** Which of the five people here do you agree with? Who do you disagree with? Compare with others in the class.

Friendship **myths**

Everyone wants to have friends, and **friendships** are important to teenagers all over the world. However, when people start a friendship, they sometimes expect too much from it. Here are five things about friendship that some people believe are true. But in fact they aren't – they are myths.

Myth no. 1: Friends are there to make you happy.

Myth no. 2: A real friend will never disappoint you.

Myth no. 3: The more friends you have, the better.

Myth no. 4: Friends share everything.

Myth no. 5: If you've got no friends, something's wrong with you.

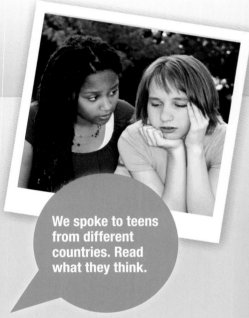

We spoke to teens from different countries. Read what they think.

Burcu, Istanbul, Turkey
Nobody's perfect, so why do we think friends can be perfect? We all make mistakes, so it's only normal that there are times when good friends make mistakes, too. Perhaps you think that a really good friend always knows what you need. That's wrong – be careful! Sometimes you need to say to your friends, 'Please do this' or 'Don't do that'. Don't forget that there are times when your friends are **stressed** or unhappy, too. Then they can't help you the way you would like them to. **1**

Flávia, São Paulo, Brazil
There can be times in your life when you've got a lot of friends, and other times when you've only got one or two. Maybe you haven't got any friends **right now** because, for example, you're in a new city or school. When you haven't got any friends, it's important to wait and **be patient**. Make sure you're a friendly person – so other people want to **make friends** with you! **2**

Fernanda, Quito, Ecuador
You want to be a good friend, right? To build a good friendship, it's important to have fun together, to listen to your friends when they've got a problem, to help them when they need you, or just to go and watch a film together, or play some sport. And that takes time! That's why I think it's better to have one or two friends, and not a lot of friends. **4**

Luca, Florence, Italy
No, they don't! It takes time to build a good friendship. You don't want to tell your friend everything about yourself on the first day of your friendship. You and your friends want to share some things. But it's important to **remember** that there are other things that you don't want to share and that's fine! Don't feel bad about it. **3**

Nikolay, St Petersburg, Russia
It's not a good idea to wait for others to make you happy. There are times when you're happy, and other times when you're sad. And when you're not happy, try to think, 'What can I do to stop this? How can I help myself?' Friendship is a place to share **happiness**, but there may be times when you and your friends aren't happy. And that's OK. **5**

4 **Read the web page again. Who says …**

1 you need to have a good time with your friends? _____

2 you won't make friends if you are an unfriendly person? _____

3 we need to remember that our friends have bad days too? _____

4 you don't have to tell your friends everything about you? _____

5 we won't always have the same number of friends in our life? _____

6 that it's not always a good thing to have a lot of friends? _____

7 we shouldn't expect our friends to always get everything right? _____

8 we shouldn't always expect friends to make us happy? _____

9 you can't always expect your friends to be happy? _____

10 you can't make a really good friend quickly? _____

5 **VOCABULARY** **There are eight words in bold in the web page. Match the words with these meanings. Write the words.**

0 an idea that many people believe, but that is not true _*myth*_

1 the state of feeling happy _____

2 the relationships you have with friends _____

3 show that you are not in a hurry and have got time _____

4 worried, for example when you have too much work _____

5 get to know and like a person _____

6 keep in your mind _____

7 at this moment _____

SPEAKING

1 **Choose the words that make the sentences true for you.**

1 When I'm sad, I want my friends to *listen to me / tell me a joke / leave me alone.*

2 When I'm happy, I want to *watch a film / play a sport / listen to music / go shopping /* with my friends.

2 **Work with a partner. Read out your sentences and compare your answers.**

WRITING
An apology

1 **Read the message and answer the questions.**

1 How does John feel and why?

2 What does he want to do about it?

> Dear Alice,
>
> I'm really sorry for forgetting your birthday. It was a terrible thing to do. I wanted to phone you but I forgot because I had a lot of work to do. I feel really bad. I'd like to see you soon to say sorry. I've also got something I want to give you.
>
> Can we meet up on Thursday?
>
> **John**

2 **Read the messages. Which is the answer to John?**

1
> Thanks for your message.
>
> Don't worry about it. I'm not upset. And yes, I'd love to see you on Thursday. I can't wait to see what you've got for me.

2
> Thanks for the message.
>
> I'm sorry I can't come to your birthday party on Thursday but I'm really busy. Have fun without me.

3 **Put the words in the right order. Write the sentences.**

1 birthday / your / really / sorry / for / I'm / forgetting

2 was / terrible / a / It / to / do / thing

3 really / I / bad / feel

4 **Match the phrases with the photos.**

eat the cake | break someone's tablet
not water the flowers

5 **Write an apology for each photo. Include an explanation with each apology.**

I'm really sorry.   *It was an accident.*

6 **Choose one of the situations from above and write a message to apologise. (60 words)**

CAMBRIDGE ENGLISH: Key

THiNK EXAMS

READING AND WRITING
Part 5: Multiple-choice cloze

Workbook page 53

1   Read the article about a strange house. Choose the best word (A, B or C) for each space.

I **(0)**_____ on holiday with my family in California a few years **(1)** _____, when Dad saw an advert for 'The Craziest House in the World' in the local paper. We decided to visit it, but on the way there we got lost. Dad **(2)** _____ want to ask anyone for directions, but after half an hour Mum told him to stop. We found a really **(3)** _____ man on a street in the town. He **(4)** _____ us a map for free! And ten minutes later, we were at the house.

From the outside, it just looked **(5)** _____ a normal big house. When we went inside we saw how **(6)** _____ it was. The house has 40 bedrooms, three lifts, 47 fireplaces and 467 doors!

It was the project of a rich American woman called Sarah Winchester. They **(7)** _____ building it in 1884 and they only stopped in 1922 when Sarah died. She never drew any plans but every time she got **(8)** _____ with the house, she just called the builders to come and build some more rooms for her.

0	A	am	B	was	C	were
1	A	last	B	before	C	ago
2	A	doesn't	B	did	C	didn't
3	A	helpful	B	jealous	C	confident
4	A	give	B	gave	C	giving
5	A	like	B	at	C	for
6	A	amazed	B	relaxing	C	amazing
7	A	start	B	started	C	starting
8	A	bored	B	boring	C	interesting

(0 B was is circled)

Part 6: Word completion

Workbook page 43

2   Complete the words.

0   You usually keep your clothes in this.
    w a r d r o b e

1   You can keep your books on this. **s** _ _ _ _ _

2   You use this to look at yourself. **m** _ _ _ _ _ _

3   Someone who knows a lot of things is this.
    i _ _ _ _ _ _ _ _ _ _ _

4   Someone who always shares their things is this.
    g _ _ _ _ _ _ _ _

5   Someone who is relaxed and doesn't worry much is this. **e** _ _ _ - _ _ _ _ _

Part 3: Dialogue matching

Workbook page 35

3   Complete the conversation between two friends. What does Nick say to Sue? For questions 1–5, write the correct letter A–H in each space.

SUE   It's Adam's birthday next week.
NICK **(0)** _F_
SUE   I think that's a great idea. But what?
NICK **(1)** _____
SUE   I don't think that's a good idea. He doesn't like reading.
NICK **(2)** _____
SUE   He downloads all his music. He hasn't even got a CD player.
NICK **(3)** _____
SUE   I'm not so sure. It's difficult to buy clothes for him.
NICK **(4)** _____
SUE   Let's invite him to the cinema. He loves films.
NICK **(5)** _____
SUE   Great. I'll get three tickets.

A   OK. Have you got any ideas?
B   We could get him a CD. He loves music.
C   Why don't we ask his dad?
D   Let's do that.
E   Why?
F   ~~Why don't we get him a present?~~
G   How about buying him a book?
H   That's true. How about a T-shirt?

LISTENING
Part 2: Matching

Workbook page 61

4   ◀)2.02 Listen to Jen telling Mark about her room. Who gave her each of the pieces of furniture? For questions 1–5, write a letter A–H next to each present.

Present

0	armchair	E
1	sofa	
2	curtains	
3	carpet	
4	desk	
5	lamp	

People

A   Dad
B   Uncle Tim
C   Aunt Abi
D   brother
E   ~~Grandpa~~
F   Uncle Simon
G   Mark
H   Mum

TEST YOURSELF

VOCABULARY

1 Use the words in the list to complete the sentences. There are two extra words.

after | make | for | really | cheerful | do | annoying | shower | last | jealous | annoyed | cooker

1 She isn't happy when I see you. I think she's a bit _____ of you.
2 I need a wash but Ian is still in the _____ .
3 Mum died when I was 14 so I helped Dad look _____ my little brothers.
4 My sister borrowed my shoes and she didn't ask me. I was really _____ .
5 I moved school when I was eight and I found it really difficult to _____ new friends.
6 I'm looking _____ Anne. Do you know where she is?
7 He's a really _____ boy. I really don't like him.
8 I had a great time _____ night – thanks for everything.
9 It's a _____ comfortable armchair. I just want to sit in it for hours.
10 Be careful – the _____ is still hot.

/10

GRAMMAR

2 Complete the sentences with the past form of the verbs in the list.

choose | find | go | think | like | see

1 I _____ he was my friend but now I'm not so sure.
2 The present was very expensive. I hope she _____ it.
3 I _____ to a party last night and I only got home at 11 pm.
4 I liked the green T-shirt but eventually I _____ the red one.
5 We _____ a dog all alone in the street so we took it home.
6 No, not that film. I _____ it last week.

3 Find and correct the mistake in each sentence.

1 I thinked you were at school.
2 Did you enjoyed your meal, Sir?
3 Paul wasn't go to school today. He stayed at home.
4 We were tired so we did go to bed early.
5 Where did you and Lucy met?
6 I wasn't hungry so I didn't ate anything.

/12

FUNCTIONAL LANGUAGE

4 Write the missing words.

1 A How a_____ inviting Jake to our party?
  B I don't think that's a good i_____ . Remember the last time he went to a party!
2 A We c_____ have pizza for lunch.
  B Let's d_____ that. I love pizza!
3 A If you need some money, w_____ don't you get a Saturday job?
  B I'm not so s_____ . I don't think my dad would like it.
4 A L_____ go to the park after school.
  B That's a g_____ idea. We can play tennis.

/8

MY SCORE /30

22 – 30
10 – 21
0 – 9

7 THE EASY LIFE

READING

1 ◆)) 2.03 **What are the objects here? Match the words in the list with the photos. Write 1–6 in the boxes. Listen, check and repeat.**

| 1 e-reader | 2 digital camera | 3 flat screen TV |
| 4 tablet | 5 laptop | 6 (desktop) computer |

2 SPEAKING **Work in pairs. Talk about the objects with a partner.**

> I've got a …
>
> I haven't got a …
>
> I think the (laptop) in the photo looks (cool / really new / quite old).

3 SPEAKING **Imagine you could only have one of these things. Which would you choose?**

> I'd choose the …
> It's important for me because …
> What about you?

4 ◆)) 2.04 **Read the sentences and guess the correct answer. Listen and check your answers.**

1 A person who **invents** something *has got an idea and creates something new / has got enough money to buy something new.*
2 If you hear something that is **shocking** it makes you feel *happy and excited / surprised and upset.*
3 I **researched** the topic *on the camera / on the Internet.*
4 What is a **huge** problem for Africa? *There is not enough clean water / There is not enough space for people.*
5 You can get **trachoma** from *dirty water / bad food.*
6 Getting an **eye infection** can make people *deaf / blind.*
7 You buy **gel** in a *plastic bottle / paper bag.*

5 SPEAKING **Work in pairs. Look at the title of the article and the photos on the next page. What do you think the article is about? Compare your ideas with other students.**

6 ◆)) 2.05 **Read and listen to the article about a young inventor. Are the sentences true (T) or false (F)? Correct the false ones.**

0 Ludwick Marishane is from South Africa. *T*
1 Ludwick used his laptop to find out more about the world's water situation.
2 Millions of people get trachoma every year.
3 Trachoma is an illness that makes people blind.
4 Ludwick wanted to help people with trachoma.
5 Ludwick's dream was to help people find clean water.
6 'DryBath' is helping to save a lot of water all over the world.
7 DryBath is a success.
8 Ludwick wants to invent more things.

'... just because I didn't want to take a bath'

LUDWICK MARISHANE, a 17-year-old South African, was with his friends in Limpopo when they started talking about inventing something to put on your skin so you don't have to take a bath. Ludwick thought that this was a great idea. He used his mobile to do some research on the Internet, and he found some shocking facts.

Two point five billion people around the world haven't got clean water. This is a huge problem because dirty water can create terrible illnesses. One of them is trachoma: eight million people all over the world get trachoma every year. They wash their faces with dirty water, get an infection and become blind. To stop trachoma, people don't have to take expensive medication. They don't have to take pills. They don't have to have injections. They have to wash their faces with clean water. That's it.

Ludwick started thinking. He wanted to make something to help people in parts of the world where it's difficult to find clean water. He did more research on his mobile, and he did more thinking. Ludwick had a plan. He wanted to make a gel for people to put on their skin so they don't have to take a bath. He wrote the formula for the gel on his mobile phone. When he was at university, he never stopped thinking about his invention. He started to talk to other people about it, and three years later the dream came true. He made the gel and called it 'DryBath'.

Ludwick Marishane is the winner of lots of prizes. People call him 'one of the brightest young men in the world'. He is very happy about his success. DryBath is helping people to be healthy. And DryBath also helps to save water. That's important in many parts of the world where it's difficult to find clean water. Now he wants to invent other things, and he wants to help other young people to become inventors too.

■ THiNK VALUES ■

Caring for people and the environment

1 Match the values in the list with the sentences in the speech bubbles. Write a–d in the boxes.

a caring about the environment
b caring about the quality of your work
c caring about your appearance
d caring about other people

1 *The water in a lot of rivers and lakes is not clean.* ☐

2 *I need to wash my hair. It's dirty.* ☐

3 *Are you feeling cold? I can give you my jumper.* ☐

4 *Can you switch off the radio, please? I'm doing my homework.* ☐

2 SPEAKING Work in pairs. Ask and answer questions about Ludwick Marishane. Try and find as many answers as possible.

*Does he care about the environment?
his appearance?
the quality of his work?
other people?*

Yes, because DryBath helps to save water.

GRAMMAR
have to / don't have to

1 Complete the sentences from the article on page 67 with *have to* and *don't have to*.

1 They _____ wash their faces with clean water.
2 To stop trachoma people _____ take expensive medication.

2 Complete the rule and the table.

> **RULE:** Use [1]_____ to say 'this is necessary'.
> Use [2]_____ to say 'this isn't necessary'.

Positive	Negative
I/you/we/they [0] **have to** help	I/you/we/they don't have to help
he/she/it [1]_____ help	he/she/it [2]_____ help

Questions	Short answers
[3]_____ I/you/we/they have to help?	Yes, I/you/we/they do. No, I/you/we/they don't.
[4]_____ he/she/it have to help?	Yes, he/she/it [5]_____ . No, he/she/it [6]_____ .

3 Match the sentences with the pictures.

1 The bus leaves in 20 minutes. He has to hurry.
2 The bus leaves in 20 minutes. He doesn't have to hurry.

4 Complete the sentences with *have to / has to* or *don't / doesn't have to*.

1 Our teacher doesn't like mobile phones. We _____ switch them off during lessons.
2 I know that I _____ work hard for this test! You _____ tell me!
3 My sister is ill. She _____ stay in bed.
4 Your room is terrible! You _____ tidy it up.
5 Mario's English is perfect. He _____ study for the tests.
6 I can hear you very well. You _____ shout!

> Workbook page 64 ➤

VOCABULARY
Gadgets

1 ◀)) 2.06 Match the words with the photos. Write 1–10 in the boxes. Then listen, check and repeat.

1 satnav | 2 MP3 player | 3 torch | 4 games console |
5 remote control | 6 coffee machine | 7 calculator |
8 docking station | 9 hair dryer | 10 headphones |

2 How important are these gadgets for you? Make a list from 1 to 10 (1 = most important, 10 = not important at all).

3 SPEAKING Work in pairs. Compare your ideas and tell your partner how often you use these gadgets.

> I often use …
>
> I use my … almost every day.
>
> What about you?
>
> I rarely use …

> Workbook page 66 ➤

LISTENING

1 **SPEAKING** Look at the pictures of different inventions. Match them with the phrases. Write 1–4 in the boxes. Then make sentences to explain what the inventions are. Compare your ideas in class.

1 not tidy up room / have got robot
2 machine help / ride bike up a hill
3 invention help homework / more time for friends
4 machine can get places around the world / 10 seconds

> The girl in picture A has got a cool machine. It helps her to ride her bike up a hill.

2 **2.07** Martin and Anna want to become inventors. Try and match the sentence parts to find out what their situation is. Then listen and check.

1 Martin has got an idea for an invention,
2 He's got a job,
3 Anna has got a lot of ideas,
4 She's thirteen,

a and wants to be an inventor.
b but doesn't want to say what it is.
c but doesn't know where to start.
d and hasn't got enough time to work on it.

3 **2.07** Complete the expert's answers with *should* or *shouldn't*. Listen again and check.

1 You _____ start thinking 'What idea can I have to make a million pounds?'
2 You _____ start with a little idea.
3 You _____ think 'What can I invent that makes one little thing in my life easier'?
4 You _____ give up your job.
5 You _____ work on your best idea first.
6 You _____ forget about your other ideas.

GRAMMAR
should / shouldn't

1 Look at the sentences in Exercise 3 of the listening. Match the sentence parts in the rule.

> **RULE:**
> 1 Use *should* to say   a 'It's not a good idea.'
> 2 Use *shouldn't* to say   b 'It's a good idea.'

2 Use *should / shouldn't* and a word from each list to give advice to these people.

~~take~~ | go to | eat | drink | read
~~aspirin~~ | book any more | bed
any more cake | water

0 I've got a headache. *You should take an aspirin.*
1 I'm really thirsty. _____
2 My eyes are tired. _____
3 I'm tired. _____
4 I feel sick. _____

→ Workbook page 64

SPEAKING

Read the sentences. Decide whether you agree or disagree. Then work in pairs. Tell your partner.

1 Students shouldn't take phones into their lessons.
2 Students should use computers in all lessons.
3 There should only be six students in a classroom.
4 Students shouldn't wear school uniforms.

> I disagree with number 2. Students should use computers in most subjects, but not in all of them. That would be boring.

READING

1 **SPEAKING** Work in pairs. Look at the pictures and think about what the machines do. Then choose one of the two machines and talk about it.

> I think it's called ... It helps with ...
> It's a cool machine because ...
> It gets angry when ...

2 Read these product reviews on a website from the year 2066. What do the robots do?

I bought the Sunny Star robot two weeks ago. It does everything for me in the morning. I don't have to do anything. It wakes me up with a nice song. I don't have to get out of bed myself. It helps me to get out of bed and carries me to the shower. Then it washes my face and brushes my teeth. It makes my bed and packs my bags for school. But you should be careful! You mustn't use it on rainy days. Sunny Star gets very angry when it rains. Then it only turns the cold water on when it puts you in the shower!

Do you like visiting other countries? Yes?

Then this invention is perfect for you. You don't have to have a lot of money. And you don't have to get up in the morning. It looks like a bed. It's got a computer. You only have to type the name of a city, and it flies you there. You can stay in bed, and you can have breakfast too. But don't tell your teachers! They would take it away from you! Oh, and there's one more thing you should know. You mustn't forget to switch Travel Plus off at night. Do you know why? Because it wants to travel day and night. It waits until you're sleeping and then it starts travelling. Then you might wake up at the North Pole or in the middle of the ocean!

3 Read the reviews again and answer the questions.

1 What's the first thing that Sunny Star does for you in the morning?
2 When does Sunny Star create problems?
3 What does Sunny Star do when it's angry?
4 What don't you have to do when you use Travel Plus?
5 Why don't you have to get up in the morning?
6 What mustn't you forget when you use Travel Plus?

GRAMMAR
mustn't / don't have to

1 Complete the sentences from the reviews. Then complete the rule with *mustn't* or *don't have to*.

1 You _____ do anything. Sunny Star does all the work for you.
2 You _____ forget to switch Travel Plus off at night.

> RULE: Use ¹_____ to say 'it's not necessary'.
> Use ²_____ to say 'don't do it! I'm telling you not to!'

2 Match sentences 1–2 with a–b.

1 You don't have to go swimming.
2 You mustn't go swimming.

a There are sharks.
b You can do something else if you prefer.

3 Complete the sentences with *mustn't* or *don't have to*.

1 A Dad, I don't want to go to the park with you.
  B No problem, Mike. You _____ be there.
2 A I'm so thirsty.
  B Stop! You _____ drink that!
3 A I'm sorry I can't join you.
  B That's fine. You _____ come.
4 A Sorry, I can't stay. I'm in a hurry.
  B Oh, no problem. You _____ wait for me.
5 A I don't like swimming.
  B We _____ go swimming. We can go to the park.
6 A The neighbour's dog is in the street. You _____ go out.
  B Thanks for telling me. I'm scared of that dog.

Workbook page 65

Pronunciation
Vowel sounds: /ʊ/ and /uː/
Go to page 121.

VOCABULARY
Housework

🔊 2.10 **Match the words with the photos. Write 1–10 in the boxes. Listen and check. Then listen again and repeat.**

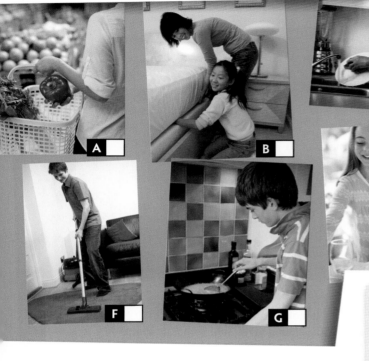

1 vacuum the floor | 2 tidy up | 3 do the ironing
4 do the shopping | 5 set / clear the table
6 do the washing-up (wash up) | 7 make the beds
8 do the cooking | 9 do the washing
10 load / empty the dishwasher

Workbook page 66 ➤

SPEAKING

1 **Read the questions. Make notes.**

1 What do you have to do at home: tidying, shopping, cooking, etc.?
2 What don't you have to do?
3 What should parents / children do at home?

2 **Plan what you are going to say. Use these phrases.**

> I have to … I think / don't think that's fair.

> I don't have to … I'm quite happy about that.
> But it would be OK for me to do that.

> I think … should do the same amount of work.
> It's not fair that …
> Mothers / Fathers should do more work because …

3 **Work in pairs or small groups. Compare your ideas about housework.**

WRITING
A paragraph about housework

Ask your partner these questions and make notes. Then write a paragraph.

1 What do you have to do at home?
2 What don't you have to do at home?
3 When do you have to do housework?
4 What do you feel about this housework?

Kate hates clearing the table, but she has to do it every evening. She also has to vacuum her bedroom floor once a week. She doesn't have to do …

▮ THiNK SELF-ESTEEM ▮
Classroom rules

1 **Write sentences about things students *have to*, *should(n't)* or *mustn't* do.**
Students have to study for their tests.
Students should speak English as much as possible.
Students mustn't leave rubbish on their desks.

2 **SPEAKING** **Compare your sentences in class. Say what you think.**

> I think it's a good idea / fair / not fair that …

> I think students / teachers / we all should(n't) …

3 **Carry out a vote to agree on the rules for your class. Make a poster, sign it and put it on the wall.**

The treasure hunt

1 🔊 **2.11 Read and listen to the photostory and answer the questions.**

Why can't Ryan come to Luke's house after school?
What's a GPS treasure hunt?

LUKE Come to my house after school.
RYAN Sorry, no chance. I have things to do.
LUKE Oh, yeah? Like what, Ryan?
RYAN Oh, homework and stuff. And I promised to help my dad with the garden. Sorry.
LUKE OK. Never mind.

1

RYAN Hey, come here, Luke. I've found something. It looks like a box. It IS a box!
LUKE What's in it? Gold coins? Diamonds? 'Ladies and gentlemen. We are now talking live to the two lucky boys who found the treasure in the park.'
RYAN You think you're really funny, Luke.
LUKE Absolutely! Come on, open the box!

2

RYAN What do we do now?
LUKE Eat it?
RYAN That sounds like a good idea. But hurry up.
LUKE What do you mean?
RYAN Look. Olivia and Megan are coming. I don't want to share it with them.

3

LUKE Hi, you two.
RYAN So, what are you up to? Using the GPS on your phone to find your way home?
MEGAN No. We're on a treasure hunt.
RYAN Sorry?
MEGAN We're trying to find some treasure. Here in the park. Using the GPS on my phone. It's such good fun!
LUKE Treasure? You mean, like a box with a little surprise in it?
OLIVIA Exactly! Now, can we keep looking?

4

DEVELOPING SPEAKING

2 Work in pairs. Discuss what happens next in the story. Write down your ideas.

We think Olivia and Megan find the box. They find ... there.

3 ▶️ **EP4** Watch to find out how the story continues.

4 Answer the questions.

1 What is Luke worried about?

2 Where does Ryan think Luke is going?

3 What's the problem with the mobile?

4 What does Olivia do to solve the problem?

5 What's the problem for Luke and Ryan?

6 What do the girls find in the box?

PHRASES FOR FLUENCY

1 Find the expressions 1–5 in the story. Who says them? How do you say them in your language?

0 no chance   *Ryan*   3 Absolutely. _____

1 ... and stuff. _____   4 So, ... ? _____

2 Never mind. _____   5 ... such good fun _____

2 Complete the dialogue with the expressions in Exercise 1.

A Do you want to come round tonight? We can play computer games ¹_____ .

B Sure. I love computer games, they're ²_____ .

A Of course. And can you bring your new laptop?

B ³_____ . It's my brother's, too. I can't take it.

A ⁴_____ . We can use mine. ⁵_____ , is seven o'clock OK?

B ⁶_____ ! See you at seven!

WordWise

Expressions with *like*

1 Complete the sentences from the story with the phrases in the list.

like | looks like | sounds like | Like what

1 Oh, yeah? _____ , Ryan?

2 It _____ a box. It IS a box.

3 That _____ a good idea.

4 Treasure? You mean, _____ a box with a little surprise in it?

2 Match the sentences.

1 This chicken isn't very good. ☐

2 Someone's talking. Who is it? ☐

3 Let's buy her a present. ☐

4 He's a really nice guy. ☐

5 What's that animal? ☐

a Like what? A poster perhaps?

b Yes, he's just like his sister, she's nice too.

c I'm not sure. It looks like a dog, but it isn't.

d That's right. It tastes like fish!

e It sounds like Jim.

3 Complete the dialogues using a phrase with *like*.

1 A I really hate tomatoes.

   B I'm _____ you. I hate them, too.

2 A Here's a photo of my sister.

   B Wow. She really _____ you!

3 A We should do some exercise.

   B _____ ? Go for a walk?

4 A Let's go to the cinema.

   B That _____ a great idea.

Workbook page 66 ➤

FUNCTIONS
Asking for repetition and clarification

1 Complete the extracts from the conversations with the words from the list.

you mean | Sorry? | Like what

LUKE   Come to my house after school.

RYAN   Sorry, no chance. I have things to do.

LUKE   ¹_____ , Ryan?

RYAN   OK, that sounds like a good idea. But hurry up!

LUKE   What do ²_____ ?

MEGAN   We're on a treasure hunt.

RYAN   ³_____

MEGAN   A GPS treasure hunt.

2 Match the expressions in Exercise 1 with their definitions.

a Say that again. _____

b What are you trying to say? _____

c Give me an example. _____

ROLE PLAY A phone call

Work in pairs. Student A: Go to page 127. Student B: Go to page 128. Take two or three minutes to prepare. Then have a conversation.

8 SPORTING MOMENTS

A

B

C

D

E

F

READING

1 Match the words in the list with the photos. Write 1–6 in the boxes.

1 basketball | 2 horse racing | 3 mountaineering
4 athletics | 5 swimming | 6 tennis

2 Which sport(s) in Exercise 1 has these things?

a ball | a race | a track | water
rope | a net | a match | a rider

3 Name other sports in English.

4 Which sports are popular in your country? Which ones do you like? Write P (popular) and/or L (like) next to each photo.

5 **SPEAKING** Compare your ideas with a partner.

> *Basketball is popular here but I don't like it very much.*

> *I like tennis and it's very popular here.*

6 Look at the photos on page 75. Answer these questions.

1 Which sports are the stories about?
2 There is something that connects both stories. What is it, do you think?

7 ◄)) **2.12** Read and listen to the article and check your answers.

8 Read the article again. Correct the information in these sentences.

1 The weather in Barcelona was bad.
2 Derek Redmond ran in the 200-metre race.
3 The race organisers tried to help Derek.
4 Derek was running when he crossed the finish line.
5 In 2010, Gerlinde Kaltenbrunner had already tried to climb K2 three times before.
6 Gerlinde was alone on the mountain.
7 The accident happened in the evening.
8 Gerlinde's dream of climbing all of the mountains in the world that are 8,000 metres or higher, is still incomplete.

IF YOU DON'T GIVE UP, YOU CAN'T FAIL ⬤ ⬤ ⬤ ⬤ ⬤

There are many stories of brave people in sport who didn't give up. Here are two of our favourites.

Derek Redmond

It was the Olympic Games in Barcelona in 1992; the semi-final of the 400 metres. The sun was shining and the crowd were ready for a great race. The British athlete Derek Redmond was a top runner: he had a very good chance of winning a medal.

The race began. At first, Derek was running well. Then, after about 150 metres, he felt a pain in his leg. He fell down on one knee. He had a bad injury and couldn't carry on. The other runners went past him and finished the race.

After about five seconds, Derek got up and started to run again, on one leg only. Some organisers tried to stop him but he kept going. The crowd stood up and started to clap. Then another man came onto the track – Derek's father, Jim. His father put his arm around him and said, 'Derek, you don't have to do this.' Derek replied, 'Yes I do. I have to finish.' And so together they walked the last 50 metres and crossed the line.

When he finally crossed the line, Derek was crying and 60,000 people were cheering him.

Gerlinde Kaltenbrunner

In the summer of 2010, mountaineer Gerlinde Kaltenbrunner was almost at the top of a mountain called K2 in Nepal. She was trying to climb the 8,611-metre mountain for the fifth time, and this time she was climbing with her friend Fredrik Ericsson.

It was about 7 o'clock in the morning and it was snowing a little. The two climbers were getting ready to go up the last 400 metres. Fredrik was trying to tie some rope but he slipped and fell past Gerlinde. He fell 1,000 metres and was killed.

Gerlinde went back to base-camp. K2 was now a very sad place for her, and she thought perhaps she would never climb the mountain.

But there was something very important that she wanted to do: K2 is one of 14 mountains in the world that are 8,000 metres or higher, and her dream was to climb them all.

So in August 2011 she went back to Nepal and K2, and tried again. This time, she got to the top. Her dream was complete.

■ THiNK VALUES ■

Trying, winning and losing

1 **Think about these sentences. Which one do you think is the most important?**

The two stories tell us that ...

1 it's important to try to win a race.
2 you shouldn't start a race if you think you can't win.
3 when you start something, you should try to finish.
4 if things go wrong, you should try to keep going.
5 if you try to climb a mountain but don't get to the top, you fail.

2 **SPEAKING** **Work in pairs. Compare your ideas with a partner.**

> I think number 1 is the most important. What about you?

GRAMMAR
Past continuous

1 Complete the sentences from the article on page 75 with the words in the list.
Then (circle) the correct words to complete the rule.

run | try | climb | shine

1 The sun _____ in Barcelona.
2 At first, Derek _____ well.
3 Gerlinde _____ with her friend Fredrik Ericsson.
4 Fredrik _____ to tie some rope.

> **RULE:** Use the past continuous to talk about *completed actions / actions in progress* at a certain time in the past.

2 Find more examples of the past continuous in the article on page 75. Then complete the table.

Positive	Negative	Questions	Short answers
I/he/she/it ¹ _____ working	I/he/she/it ³ _____ (was not) working	⁴ _____ I/he/she/it working?	Yes, I/he/she/ it ⁶ _____ . No, I/he/she/it ⁷ _____ (was not).
you/we/they ² _____ working	you/we/they weren't (were not) working	⁵ _____ you/we/ they working?	Yes, you/we/they/ ⁸ _____ . No, you/we/they ⁹ _____ (were not).

Pronunciation

Strong and weak forms of *was* and *were*

Go to page 121.

3 Yesterday the sports teacher was late. What were the students doing when he got there? Complete the sentences with the correct form of the verbs in brackets.

0 Lucy _*was talking*_ (talk) on her phone.
1 Daniel and Sophie _____ (play) basketball.
2 Samuel _____ (read) a book.
3 Ken _____ (climb) up a rope.
4 Lisa _____ (dream) about a day on the beach.
5 Andy _____ (look) at his photos on his tablet.

4 Complete the dialogues with the past continuous form of the verbs.

1 A What _____ (you/do) yesterday when we phoned you?
  B I _____ (wait) for my mother in town. And it was horrible because it _____ (rain)!

2 A Why didn't you answer when I phoned you?
  B I _____ (cook) my lunch.

3 A Was it a good game yesterday?
  B Well, the beginning was fine. We _____ (play) well and we _____ (win). But then they scored four goals!

4 A _____ (you/watch) TV when I called last night?
  B No, I wasn't. I _____ (read) a magazine.

Workbook page 72

VOCABULARY
Sports and sports verbs

1 Match the words in the list with the photos. Write 1–10 in the boxes.

1 sailing | 2 diving | 3 golf | 4 gymnastics
5 rock-climbing | 6 rugby | 7 snowboarding
8 skiing | 9 volleyball | 10 windsurfing

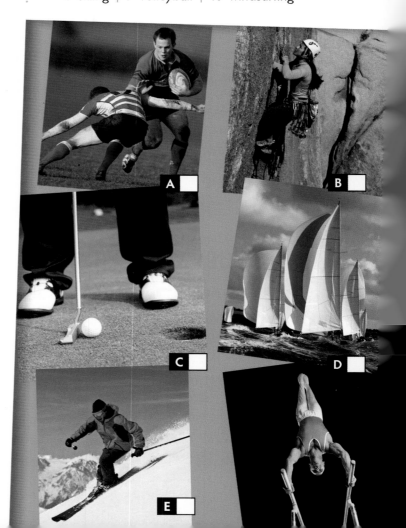

A ☐   B ☐

C ☐   D ☐

E ☐

2 **Answer the questions.**

1 Two of the sports in Exercise 1 have *players* and a *team*. Which ones are they?

2 Seven of the sports in Exercise 1 add *-er* or *-or* for the people who do them. Which ones are they?

3 What do we call someone who does gymnastics?

3 **We use different verbs for different kinds of sports. Read the rule and then complete the table with the sports in Exercise 1.**

> **RULE:**
>
> *play* + game (e.g. *football*)
> *go* + *-ing* (e.g. *running*)
> *do* + activity (e.g. *athletics*)

play	*go*	*do*
football	*running*	*athletics*

4 **SPEAKING** **Work in groups. Answer the questions about the sports in Exercise 1.**

Which sports …

1 are team sports?

2 are dangerous?

3 are water sports?

4 are in the Winter Olympics?

5 are expensive?

6 are difficult to play or do?

> Workbook page 74

LISTENING

1 **◁)) 2.15** **Five teenagers were asked the question: 'How do you feel about sport?' Listen and tick (✓) the sport(s) that each one mentions.**

	Gemma	Andy	Tracey	Paul	Ryan
football					
swimming					
running					
skateboarding					
gymnastics					
skiing					
tennis					

2 **◁)) 2.15** **Listen again. Who expresses these ideas? Write the name.**

1 I practise a lot. _____

2 I am not competitive. _____

3 I like doing things alone. _____

4 I'm learning another sport. _____

5 I can't do my sport at school. _____

3 **SPEAKING** **Work in pairs. Which of the five teenagers are you like? Tell your partner.**

> *I'm like Gemma because I don't really like sport.*

> *I really like running, so I'm like Andy.*

FUNCTIONS
Talking about feelings

1 **You are going to answer the question: 'How do you feel about sport?' List some sports you want to talk about.**

running, football, swimming, surfing

2 **What do you want to say about each sport? Mark them ✓ for positive comments; and ✗ for negative ones.**

running ✗   football ✗   swimming ✓   surfing ✓

3 **Think about why you put ✓ or ✗. Look at the words and ideas in Vocabulary, Exercise 4. Use these words and / or other words you know.**

running ✗ boring   football ✗ team sport
swimming ✓ fun   surfing ✓ difficult and fun

4 **Work in pairs. Ask each other: 'How do you feel about sport?'**

> *How do you feel about sport?*

> *Well I don't like running because it's boring. But swimming is fun and I love surfing because it's fun and it's difficult to do.*

G

H

I

J

42

READING

1 Look at the pictures. What do you think is happening in each one?

A

B

C

D

2 Read the stories and match them with the pictures. Write the numbers 1–4 in the boxes.

3 Read the stories again. Answer the questions.

1 Why does Alan think the story about the bird is funny?
2 Why didn't the girl see the ball coming at her?
3 What happened to the referee?
4 Why did the cyclist lose control of the bike?

4 SPEAKING How funny do you think these stories are? Give each one a number from 0–5 (0 = not funny at all, 5 = very, very funny). Compare your ideas with a partner.

■ TRAIN TO THiNK ■

Sequencing

1 Look at the lists. Put them in a logical order.

1 morning – night – afternoon – evening
2 tomorrow – today – next week – yesterday
3 Saturday – Wednesday – Monday – Friday
4 have lunch – come home – go to school – wake up
5 baby – adult – child – teenager
6 first half – kick-off – half-time – second half

2 SPEAKING Compare your ideas with other students. Are they the same or different?

Your favourite sports FAILS!

1 ALAN Today 4 pm
I saw a really funny thing on YouTube the other day. It was a tennis match. Four people were playing – it was in a big competition. One of the players was hitting the ball when a bird flew in – and the ball hit the bird and it fell to the ground. The players stopped and one of them picked the bird up – they thought it was dead. But suddenly the bird flew away again and they all laughed!

2 JILLY Today 1 pm
I was watching an American football game, a long time ago. There were some girls who were standing at the side of the ground. One player threw the ball really hard – and very badly! One of the girls was looking the other way when the ball hit her. She just didn't see it – and it knocked her over. Everyone was worried; the player went to see if she was OK – then she stood up and laughed and the player gave her a big hug.

3 MARK Today 10 am
I love sumo wrestling – you know, the big Japanese men who wrestle in a small ring. I was watching some on TV, and one wrestler started pushing the other one. He was pushing and pushing and they started to fall over, and the little referee was there behind them – he was trying to get out of the way but then the two men fell on him and he fell out of the ring!

4 PAULA Today 9 am
I went to watch a cycling race the other day. I was standing at the finishing line, and I saw the first cyclist come round the corner to finish the race. At first, he was very happy because he was winning – but he wasn't at the finishing line yet! While he was still cycling, he put his arms up in the air to celebrate. After two seconds, he lost control of the bike. And finally he fell off! He got back on the bike but another cyclist went past him, so in the end he came second. Poor guy – but it was his fault!

GRAMMAR
Past continuous vs. past simple

1 Look at these sentences from the stories on page 78. <u>Underline</u> the past continuous verb and circle the past simple forms.

1 One of the players was hitting the ball when a bird flew in.

2 One girl was looking the other way when the ball hit her.

3 He was trying to get out of the way but the two men fell on him.

4 While he was still cycling, he put his arms up in the air.

2 Look at the diagram. Which part of the sentence tells us the background action? Which part of the sentence tells us what happened at one moment? Complete the rule.

One of the players **was hitting** the ball

⟶

a bird **flew** in. ↑

> **RULE:** Use the ¹_____ to talk about background actions in the past, and the ²_____ for actions which happened at one moment (and sometimes interrupted the background action).

3 Complete the sentences. Use the past continuous or past simple form of the verbs.

0 He _was running_ (run) and he suddenly _felt_ (feel) a pain in his leg.

1 The ball _____ (hit) me while I _____ (watch) a bird.

2 Jenny _____ (sail) with her father when she _____ (see) some dolphins.

3 He _____ (chase) the ball and he _____ (fall) over.

4 When I _____ (look) out of the window, it _____ (snow).

5 The electricity _____ (go) off while we _____ (watch) a match on TV.

4 Complete the text with the correct form of the verbs.

A few years ago, in a football match in England between Chelsea and Liverpool, a strange thing happened. Chelsea ¹_____ (win) the match 2–1 and there were about twenty minutes left. Two players – Luis Suárez and Branislav Ivanović – ²_____ (run) after the ball. While they ³_____ (try) to get to the ball, Suárez suddenly ⁴_____ (take) Ivanović's arm and ⁵_____ (bite) it! The referee ⁶_____ (not see) it happen so Suárez ⁷_____ (continue) playing.

when and while

5 Look at the sentences in Exercises 3 and 4. Complete the rule.

> **RULE:** We often use **when** before the past ¹_____ and **while** before the past ²_____ .

6 Complete the sentences. Use the past continuous for the longer activity and the past simple for the shorter one.

0 I _was writing_ (write) an email. My phone _rang_ (ring).

1 Alex and Sue _____ (watch) a film on DVD. Their friends _____ (arrive).

2 Marco _____ (have) breakfast. He _____ (have) a great idea.

3 Cristina _____ (talk) on the phone. Her father _____ (go) out.

4 They _____ (walk) in the mountains. They _____ (see) strange bird.

7 Join the sentences in Exercise 6 in two different ways. Use *when* and *while*.

*I was writing an email **when** my phone rang.*
***While** I was writing an email, my phone rang.*

> **Workbook page 73** ▸

VOCABULARY
Adverbs of sequence

1 Match the parts of the sentences.

1 At first,   a two seconds, he lost control of the bike.

2 Then   b he was very happy.

3 After   c he fell off.

4 Finally,   d he put his arms up to celebrate.

2 Complete the story with the words in Exercise 1.

¹_____ , I was very nervous. ²_____ the starter fired the gun.

³_____ ten seconds, I crossed the finish line and won! I was the Olympic champion!

⁴_____ the photographers took photos of me. ⁵_____ an hour, they gave me the gold medal.

⁶_____ , I woke up.

> **Workbook page 74** ▸

Culture

1 **Look at the pictures and answer the questions. Then say what you think the article is about.**

Where can you see the following things?
- a marathon race
- an athlete
- spectators
- the finishing line

2 **◀)) 2.16** **Read and listen to the article. Match the pictures with the correct Olympic Games.**

3 **SPEAKING** **Which Olympic moment do you like most? Which do you not like? Compare your ideas with others in the class.**

THE OLYMPIC GAMES – the good and the not-so-good

The Olympic Games takes place every four years and usually there is something special that people never forget. Here are some of those moments from the past – some good, some not so good.

1908 London – the marathon
At the end of the marathon, the man who was winning – Dorando Pietri, from Italy – was very tired and fell down four times. People picked him up and he crossed the line – so of course he didn't win the gold medal because people helped him. But he became very famous.

1960 Rome – a winner with no shoes
The winner of the marathon in Rome was Abebe Bikila from Ethiopia. A lot of other runners (and some of the spectators – the people in the stadium) laughed when they first saw him – he had no shoes. They weren't laughing at the end when Bikila won the gold medal. (He won in 1964 in Tokyo too – but wearing shoes.)

1968 Mexico – a big jump
Mexico City is very high and the air is thin – which was a good thing for some athletes, not so good for others. One special moment was the long jump – Bob Beamon of the USA jumped 8.9 metres. Beamon's jump was the World Record for 23 years.

1996 Atlanta – a bomb
During the 1996 Olympic Games, something very sad happened. A bomb exploded in a park near the Olympic stadium. One person was killed, and 111 people were taken to hospital.

2000 Sydney – the Green Games
The Sydney Olympic Games were called 'The Green Games' because all the buildings (the stadium, the houses for the athletes, etc.) were built to be as friendly as possible to the environment. Many people thought these Olympic Games were the best ever.

2004 Athens – another marathon story
In the men's marathon, after about 35 kilometres, Brazilian Vanderlei de Lima was running very fast. He was first, and the second runner was 40 seconds behind him. But then an Irishman ran out from the crowd and pushed him. Other people in the crowd stopped the Irishman. Then de Lima started to run again. He was smiling when he finished the marathon third – he won the bronze medal.

2012 London – a bottle-thrower
It was the final of the men's 100 metres. All the athletes were ready to start the race. Suddenly a man in the crowd threw a plastic bottle at the athletes. But they were lucky. The bottle didn't hit any of them. The race started. A Dutch woman was sitting next to the man. She grabbed him so he couldn't run away. The woman, Edith Bosch, was a bronze-medal winner in judo at the Games.

A   B   C

4 **Read the article again and answer the questions.**

Who ...

1 had help to finish the race?
2 raced barefoot?
3 was stopped in the middle of his race?
4 caught a criminal?
5 won gold in two different Olympics?
6 came 3rd in an event at the London Olympics?
7 finished first but didn't get a medal?
8 broke an Olympic record?
9 won a marathon bronze medal?

5 VOCABULARY **There are eight highlighted words in the article. Match the words with these meanings. Write the words.**

0	took quickly in their hands	*grabbed*
1	the prize given to the athletes that come third in a race at the Olympics	_____
2	a 42.2 km race	_____
3	happens	_____
4	the prize given to the winners at the Olympic games	_____
5	a competition where athletes run to see who is the fastest	_____
6	people who watch a race or game	_____
7	went from one side to the other side	_____

WRITING
An article about a sporting event

1 **Read Max's article in a school magazine about going to an important tennis match. Answer the questions.**

1 Who did Max go with?
2 Who did Max think would win?
3 Who won?
4 What did Max do after the match?

2 **Find these words in the article. What does each word describe? Why does Max use them?**

0 lucky   *my family*

1 full   _____   4 great   _____
2 excited   _____   5 fantastic   _____
3 unhappy   _____

3 **Look at the three paragraphs of Max's article. Match the paragraphs with the contents.**

Paragraph 1   a after the event
Paragraph 2   b introduction to the event
Paragraph 3   c details of the event (the match itself)

4 **Think of a sports event that you went to or would like to go to. Answer the questions.**

1 When is / was the event?
2 Where is / was it?
3 What is / was the atmosphere like (the crowd and the noise, etc.)?
4 What happens / happened at the event? (players / goals / winners, etc.)
5 How did / would you feel after the event? (happy? tired? excited? unhappy?)

5 **Write an article for a school magazine (about 120–150 words) about the sports event. Use Max's article and the language above to help you.**

SPORTS NEWS

(1) Last Saturday was the final of the women's singles at the Wimbledon Tennis Championships, played (of course) at the Wimbledon Tennis Club. My family were lucky enough to get tickets. When we got there, we went to the court and found our seats. Of course the stadium was full and everyone was very excited. It was brilliant!

(2) At ten to two, the players came out: Marion Bartoli from France and Sabine Lisicki from Germany. At first, I was sure Lisicki was going to win but when the match started, it was clear that I was wrong. Bartoli played really well and after thirty minutes, the first set ended: 6–1 to Bartoli. And twenty-five minutes later, the second set was 5–1 to Bartoli. Lisicki was very unhappy but she started to play better, and soon it was 5–4. Could Lisicki come back? No. Bartoli hit great shots and won the second set 6–4. The crowd stood and clapped and cheered. And then Bartoli got the trophy.

(3) When the match ended, we looked around a bit and then went home. We had a great time. Maybe the match wasn't the most exciting ever, but it was fantastic to see a big sports event 'live'.

THiNK EXAMS

READING AND WRITING
Part 1: Matching
Workbook page 71

1 Which notice (A–H) says this (1–5)? Write the letters A–H.

0	Adults only.	*C*
1	You don't have to pay if you're eight.	
2	You shouldn't leave your car here.	
3	The shop closes in the afternoon.	
4	You should call for more information.	
5	You mustn't swim here.	

Please phone for more details. **A**

• Museum • FREE to children under nine **B**

You have to be over **18** to watch this film. **C**

Please DON'T park in front of our shop. **D**

OPENING HOURS 9 am – 11.30 am **E**

DANGEROUS DEEP WATER KEEP OUT **F**

CLOSED on Saturdays **G**

Parking £2 per hour **H**

Part 3: Multiple-choice replies
Workbook page 17

2 Complete five conversations. Choose the correct answer A, B or C.

0 It's not cold today.
- A You mustn't wear shorts.
- B You must wear a jacket.
- (C) You don't have to wear a jumper.

1 It's very dark. I can't see anything.
- A You need some headphones.
- B Here's a torch for you.
- C I've got a docking station, if you want.

2 I've got a headache.
- A You should go to bed for half an hour.
- B You should watch TV.
- C You shouldn't get some rest.

3 Let's go sailing tomorrow.
- A I can't. I haven't got a bike.
- B OK, I've got a ball.
- C Sorry, I don't like water.

4 Where were you at 3 pm?
- A I am watching TV.
- B I walked in the park.
- C I was playing basketball.

5 Do you want to go to the cinema?
- A No, I have to.
- B Sorry. I've got to tidy up.
- C Yes, I must.

LISTENING
Part 4: Note taking
Workbook page 79

3 🔊 2.17 You will hear a man asking for information about a football match. Listen and complete each question.

Football match

Day of game:	0	*Sunday*
Game starts:	1	_____
Family ticket:	2	£ _____
Food:	3	Hot drinks and _____
Buy tickets at:	4	Club shop in _____ Street

TEST YOURSELF

VOCABULARY

1 Complete the sentences with the words in the list. There are two extra words.

calculator | sailing | remote control | coffee machine | does | headphones
volleyball | up | windsurfing | satnav | make | skiing

1 We're lost. We need a _____ .
2 I have to _____ my bed every morning before I go to school.
3 What a mess. Someone should do the washing- _____ .
4 I love _____ . I've got a small boat and I go every weekend.
5 What is 7% of 270? I need a _____ .
6 I was playing _____ when the ball hit me on the head.
7 Pass me the _____ , please. I want to watch the news.
8 My mum was _____ and she fell over in the snow three times!
9 Dad _____ the cooking in my house.
10 I'm trying to work and your music is too loud. Can you wear _____ ?

/10

GRAMMAR

2 Complete the sentences with the past simple or past continuous form of the verbs.

see | walk | stop | eat | find | play

1 She _____ her dog when I saw her.
2 I was tidying my room when I _____ my favourite pen that I lost last week.
3 The docking station _____ working while we were listening to music.
4 We started running when we _____ the bus.
5 I _____ my dinner when the phone rang.
6 We _____ football when Mum called us for dinner.

3 Find and correct the mistake in each sentence.

1 My mum and my dad was playing in the sand with my sister.
2 You not have to go if you don't want to.
3 We mustn't run. The train doesn't go for an hour.
4 You must to be careful. It's very dangerous.
5 I played football when I broke my leg.
6 Yesterday the sports shop was sell them for only £15.

/12

FUNCTIONAL LANGUAGE

4 Write the missing words.

1 **A** You _____ have to eat it if you don't want to.
   B Thanks, I don't _____ like it.
2 **A** I can't come to your house. I've got lots of things to do.
   B Like _____ ?
   A Well, I've got to help my dad _____ the shopping, for a start.
3 **A** At _____ I was a bit scared but _____ a while I was OK.
4 **A** What _____ you doing at nine o'clock?
   B I was _____ the washing-up.

/8

MY SCORE /30

| 22 – 30 |
| 10 – 21 |
| 0 – 9 |

9 THE WONDERS OF THE WORLD

THE WONDERS OF THE WORLD

OBJECTIVES

FUNCTIONS: paying compliments; talking about the weather

GRAMMAR: comparative adjectives; superlative adjectives; can / can't for ability

VOCABULARY: geographical features; the weather; Phrases with *with*

An amazing place

They eat wild animals, plants, berries, nuts and insects. They hunt with bows and arrows. There are lots of dangerous snakes, spiders and scorpions. There are lions, leopards, cheetahs and hyenas. It's one of southern Africa's hottest places, and there is often no water. Then they have to get their water from plants, for example from desert melons. When they are ill, there are no hospitals. The people have to get their medicine from plants too.

They are the San, the last people living in the Kalahari. The San people have another name – 'bush people'. Their lifestyle is very simple, but they know more about animals and plants than most people do. The San people live in small groups of 25–50. They live in huts – little 'houses' that they make from wood and grass. There are no schools for the children. Children learn from the older people in the group. There are lots of things they have to learn so that they can live in a dangerous place like the Kalahari. In the evenings, the groups of people often sit around a fire and tell stories. Many of the stories are about animals and how to hunt them.

The Kalahari is a big area of bushland in southern Africa. It has got two parts. There is less rain in the southern part than there is in the northern part, so the south is drier. There are fewer plants and animals there, and it's a lot more difficult for people to live. But when it rains at the end of the summer, the land becomes greener and more beautiful. For a few weeks, there are millions of little flowers and even butterflies! But soon, the grass and the bushes get dry and turn brown. Then life becomes more difficult again for people and animals.

READING

1 Look at the photos. Which of the animals can you name in English?

2 Name other animals in English. Write them down.

3 **SPEAKING** Work in pairs. Look at the animals on your list. What countries do you think of?

> Pandas come from China.

> You find spiders all over the world.

4 **SPEAKING** Work in pairs. Look at the photos again and answer the questions.

1 What do the photos show?
2 Where do these people live?
3 What do you think they eat?
4 What dangers are there?
5 What do these people know a lot about?
6 What's interesting for tourists about this place?

5 **2.18** Read and listen to the article. Mark the statements T (True) or F (False). Correct the false information.

1 The bush people get their water from the river.
2 When the San people are ill, they get medicine from a hospital.
3 The bush people teach children important things about living in the Kalahari.
4 The north of the Kalahari is wetter than the south.
5 There are more animals and plants in northern Kalahari.
6 A holiday in the Kalahari is never dangerous.

Every year, thousands of tourists from all over the world visit the Kalahari. They love driving around the bushland in open jeeps. They love watching the wild animals. Their guides are often San bushmen and the tourists love listening to their stories about the wonders of the Kalahari. The tourists stay in small huts called 'lodges'. They have comfortable beds and showers, but there is no electricity in the huts. When they go out of their hut, they have to be very careful. Sometimes there are lions or leopards around!

6 **SPEAKING** Work in pairs or small groups. Think about and answer these questions.

1 Would you like to go to the Kalahari? Why (not)?
2 Are you interested in wildlife? Why (not)?

> I'd love to / I wouldn't like to ... because ...

> I'm (not) interested in ...

> I think it's too dangerous to ... / wonderful to ...

> I love / hate taking photos. watching ... / staying in ...

■ THiNK VALUES ■

Valuing our world

1 Read and tick (✓) the statements that show that the natural world is important.

1 Why should I want to go on a safari? There's a nice zoo in my city where I can see lots of animals.

2 I want to build a hotel for 800 people in the Kalahari Desert. We can make a lot of money like that.

3 It's great to learn about wild animals. It helps me to understand more about the world.

4 Who needs lions, leopards and hyenas? They're dangerous animals and that's it!

5 I watch a lot of nature programmes on TV. I support a project to save the tiger in India.

2 **SPEAKING** Compare your ideas in pairs.

> Statement 1 shows that the natural world is not important for this person.

> Why do you think that?

> Because the person doesn't want to see wild animals in nature.

> But maybe that's not true. Maybe he or she thinks flying to other places is not good for nature.

GRAMMAR
Comparative adjectives

1 **Look at the article on page 84. Find examples of comparisons. Then complete the table on the right.**

2 **Complete the sentences. Use the comparative form of the adjectives.**

1 Africa is _____ (big) than Europe, but _____ (small) than Asia.

2 Be careful with the spiders in the Kalahari. They're _____ (dangerous) than in Europe.

3 Cars these days are _____ (good) quality than they were 30 years ago.

4 Sarah loves wildlife. For her, holidays in the Kalahari are _____ (interesting) than going to the seaside.

5 My sister has got two children. Her son is nine. His sister is two years _____ (young).

6 John is a musician. It's _____ (easy) for him to learn a new instrument than it is for me.

	adjectives	comparative form
short adjectives (one syllable)	small big hot	0 _**smaller**_ (than) bigger (than) 1 _____
adjectives ending in consonant + -y	happy dry early	happier (than) 2 _____ (than) 3 _____ (than)
longer adjectives (two or more syllables)	attractive beautiful	4 _____ (than) more beautiful (than)
irregular adjectives	bad good far	worse (than) 5 _____ (than) farther / further (than)

Workbook page 82 ▸

VOCABULARY
Geographical features

1 🔊2.19 **Label the picture with the words. Write 1–12 in the boxes. Then listen, check and repeat.**

1 ocean | **2** hill | **3** mountain | **4** jungle | **5** river | **6** desert | **7** lake | **8** beach | **9** island | **10** forest

2 **SPEAKING Work in pairs. Ask your partner to close their book and then ask them about the picture.**

> What's A?

> I think it's ... / I'm not sure if I can remember. Is it ... ? / Can you give me the first letter, please?

3 **SPEAKING Work in pairs. Compare some of the places. Use the adjectives in the list to help you, or use other adjectives.**

hot | big | dangerous | high | nice
difficult | beautiful | exciting

> A mountain is higher than a hill.

> Yes, and it's more difficult to climb a mountain.

Workbook page 84 ▸

LISTENING

1 **Match the things in the list with the photos. Write 1–4 in the boxes.**

1 vultures | 2 a lion and its kill | 3 a spear | 4 an antelope

2 🔊2.20 **Listen to an interview with a bushman from the Kalahari. Choose the title that best sums up what he talks about.**

1 Life in the Kalahari
2 Lions, vultures and antelopes
3 A difficult task for a young man
4 Big cats can't run fast when it's hot

3 🔊2.20 **Listen again.**
For questions 1–5, tick (✓) A, B or C.

1 Where was PK born?
A in the Kalahari ☐
B in the Sahara ☐
C in Kenya ☐

2 Before a young man can get married, he has to
A do a task. ☐
B find a lion. ☐
C kill an antelope. ☐

3 It's important for the future family that the young man
A kills many lions. ☐
B likes the girl's father. ☐
C has courage. ☐

4 What can show the bushman where the lion is eating?
A antelopes ☐
B vultures ☐
C his future family ☐

5 To take the kill away from the lion you have to
A run faster than the lion can. ☐
B attack the lion with your spear. ☐
C be very quiet and surprise the lion. ☐

GRAMMAR
can / can't for ability

1 **Look at the examples. How do you say these sentences in your language?**

1 A man **can** run even when it's very hot.
2 Lions **can't** do that.

2 **Look at these sentences from the interview. Complete them with can or can't.**

1 How _____ you find a lion and its kill?
2 You _____ get the kill from the lion at night.
3 How _____ you take the meat away from the lion?

3 **Complete the table.**

Positive	I/you/we/they/he/she/it **can** run fast.
Negative	I/you/we/they/he/she/it [1]_____ (**cannot**) run fast.
Questions	[2]_____ I/you/we/they/he/she/it run fast?
Short answers	Yes, I/you/we/they/he/she/it **can**. No, I/you/we/they/he/she/it [3]_____ (**cannot**).

4 **Make sentences with can and can't.**

0 Simon + run fast / – swim fast
  Simon can run fast but he can't swim fast.
1 Matt + drive a car / – fly a plane
  Matt _____
2 Dogs + understand humans / – speak
  Dogs _____
3 I + write emails / – do maths on my laptop
  I _____
4 They + write stories / – spell well
  They _____

> Workbook page 82 ➤

■ THiNK SELF-ESTEEM ■

Being brave is …

SPEAKING **Think about and answer these questions. Compare your ideas with a partner.**

1 In what situations do people have to show courage?
2 When is it difficult to show courage?
3 Who could be a role model for you in situations where you need to show courage?

> People have to show courage when they are in new situations.

> It's difficult to show courage when you're scared.

READING

1 Read the article. Where's the world's driest place?

Could you live there?

Death Valley, California

Italy

Antarctica

1 The hottest place on Earth
Death Valley is one of the world's hottest areas, but the place with the record for the highest temperature is El Aziziya in Libya. There, the temperature reached a record of 57.8°C in 1922. Death Valley's highest temperature on record is 56.7°C. That's not a lot cooler!

2 Antarctica – the place with the most weather records
Antarctica is the most fascinating place for extreme weather. It's the world's coldest place. And it's the wettest, but also the driest place. Are you surprised? Well, here are the facts. People cannot live in Antarctica all year round because it's too cold. In 1983 scientists recorded the lowest temperature ever: -89.4°C! It's also the wettest place on earth, but not because it's got the most rain or snow. It's the 'wettest' place because 98% of Antarctica is covered in ice. But it's also the driest place because it never rains there – it only snows! Antarctica holds another record too – there is a place there with the world's thickest ice; it's 2,555 m deep!

3 The world's best and worst weather
So where are the best and worst places in the world for weather? That's the most difficult question. What's good for one person may be bad for another. In 2012 an organisation named 'International Living' tried to answer this – their number 1 for the best weather was Italy, their number 2 was France, and Mexico was number 3! Where do you think your country would come?

2 Read the article again. Answer the questions.

1 Which is hotter, El Aziziya or Death Valley?
2 What place holds the most weather records?
3 Why is it difficult to say where the world's best and worst weather is?

SPEAKING

Work in pairs. Discuss these questions.

1 Which of the facts did you know before?
2 Which of the facts were new to you?
3 Which of the places mentioned would you like to visit most? Why?
4 What's your answer to the question at the end of the article? Give your reasons.

Pronunciation

Vowel sounds: /ɪ/ and /aɪ/

Go to page 121.

WRITING
An email about a place

Imagine you want to tell a friend about the place in the article that you find most interesting. Write an email (100–125 words).

- Choose the place.
- In your email, say:
  – where the place is
  – what's special about the weather there
  – why you think it's interesting

GRAMMAR
Superlative adjectives

1 Put the words in order to make sentences. Check your answers in the article.

1 world's / hottest / is / of / Death Valley / the / places / one
2 for / the / is / most fascinating / Antarctica / extreme / place / weather
3 coldest / the / place / world's / It's
4 the / Where / weather? / are / and / best / for / worst / places

2 **Look at the table. Complete the 'adjectives' column with the words in the list. Then complete the comparative and superlative forms.**

~~low~~ | fascinating | happy | bad | hot

	adjectives	comparative form	superlative form
short adjectives (one syllable)	0 _low_ high thick	lower 5 _____ 6 _____	the lowest 14 _____ 15 _____
short adjectives ending in one vowel + one consonant	1 _____ wet	hotter 7 _____	16 _____ 17 _____
adjectives ending in consonant + -y	dry 2 _____	8 _____ happier	18 _____ 19 _____
longer adjectives (two or more syllables)	3 _____ difficult extreme	more fascinating 9 _____ 10 _____	the most fascinating 20 _____ 21 _____
irregular adjectives	4 _____ good far	11 _____ 12 _____ 13 _____	the worst 22 _____ 23 _____

3 **Complete the sentences. Use the superlative form of the adjectives.**

0 It's Cindy's birthday tomorrow. She's __the happiest__ (happy) girl in class.

1 Brazil is _____ (big) country in South America.

2 I had an awful headache this morning. I think I did _____ (bad) test ever.

3 I think email is _____ (good) way of contacting people.

4 We all live a long way from school, but Sam lives the _____ (far).

5 She's great at Maths. She can solve _____ (difficult) puzzles.

Workbook page 83 ➤

VOCABULARY
The weather

1 **◄))2.23** **Write the words under the pictures. Listen and check.**

freezing | sunny | rainy | humid | windy | wet | cloudy | dry | warm | foggy | cold | hot

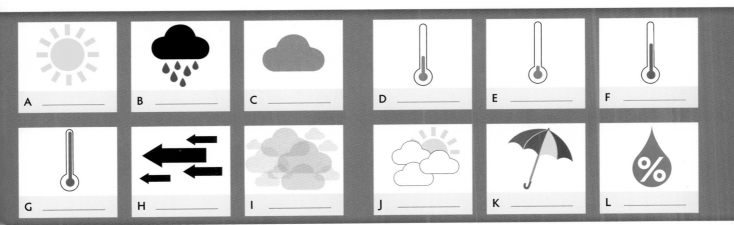

A _____ B _____ C _____ D _____ E _____ F _____

G _____ H _____ I _____ J _____ K _____ L _____

2 **Think about the different kinds of weather. Write reasons why you think they can be good.**

a sunny day: We can ride our bikes.
a hot day: We can go swimming.
a rainy day: We can play computer games.

3 **SPEAKING** **Work in pairs. Make dialogues with a partner.**

What a nice day.

Great idea.

Yes, it's really warm. Let's ride our bikes.

Workbook page 84 ➤

The competition

1 🔊 2.24 **Look at the photos and answer the questions. Then read and listen and check your answers.**

What competition is Mr Lane entering?
Why is Megan upset?

OLIVIA Hi, guys. Where's Megan?
RYAN She's not with us.
OLIVIA That's strange. I'm sure she said three o'clock.
RYAN Well, it's a nice day. Maybe she went swimming?
LUKE It's only quarter past now. She'll be here in a minute.

RYAN Hi, Mr Lane. How are you?
MR LANE I'm OK – a bit busy with this Prettiest Park Competition.
OLIVIA Prettiest Park Competition? What's that?
MR LANE It's a competition to choose the best park in the city.

MR LANE We did really well last year. We came second.
RYAN Oh! Well done!
LUKE But this year you want to do better.
MR LANE Of course. I want to show the judges that my park is the most beautiful one in the city.
LUKE Well, good luck. I hope you win.
MR LANE Thanks. It's a lot of work though, and I haven't got much time. And no one to help me, either.

MEGAN Sorry I'm late.
OLIVIA No problem. Are you all right?
MEGAN Not really. I was at my granddad's new place. He's pretty upset about having to move. He really misses his garden.
LUKE Does he like gardening, then?
MEGAN Like it?! He loves it!

DEVELOPING SPEAKING

2 Work in pairs. Discuss what happens next in the story. Write down your ideas.

We think the four friends all go to see Megan's granddad's garden.

3 ◼️ EP5 Watch to find out how the story continues.

4 Put the events in the right order.

a Megan's grandfather meets Mr Lane.

b Megan and Luke go and see her grandfather. [1]

c They admire the garden.

d Megan's grandfather shows the trophy to Megan, Luke, Ryan and Olivia.

e Luke tells Megan's grandfather about the competition.

f Mr Lane and Megan's grandfather work in the park.

PHRASES FOR FLUENCY

1 Find the expressions 1–5 in the story. Who says them? How do you say them in your language?

0 … in a minute. *Luke*   3 No problem. _____

1 Well done! _____   4 Not really. _____

2 … , either. _____   5 … , then? _____

2 Complete the conversations with the expressions in Exercise 1.

1 A I got 87% in the test, Dad.

   B _____ ! Did you study hard for it, _____ ?

2 A Hi, James. I can't talk right now. Sorry. I'll phone you _____ , OK?

   B _____ , Steve. Call me back when you can.

3 A Did you enjoy the film?

   B No, _____ . I didn't like the book very much, _____ .

WordWise
Phrases with *with*

1 Complete the sentences from the story with the phrases in the list.

busy with | to do with me | with us

1 Megan? She's not _____ .

2 I'm a bit _____ the competition.

3 What's this got _____ ?

2 Match the parts of the sentences.

1 You kill the lion [ ]

2 It's a paradise [ ]

3 We don't offer you a hotel [ ]

4 Are you good [ ]

a with the biggest rooms.

b with your spear.

c with animals?

d with 200 different kinds of birds.

3 Complete the sentences with the phrases in Exercises 1 and 2.

0 He lives in a house ___with___ four bedrooms.

1 Sorry, I can't talk now, I'm _____ my homework.

2 We went to the lake and some friends came _____ .

3 I'm sorry you lost your book, but it hasn't got anything _____ .

4 Have you got a problem with your cat? Talk to John – he's _____ cats.

Workbook page 84 ➡️

1

2

3

FUNCTIONS
Paying compliments

1 Put the words in order to make compliments.

1 a / garden / beautiful / What

2 wonderful / a / garden / It's

3 I / flowers / blue / those / love

2 Work in pairs. Use the photos to make compliments.

What a lovely picture!

10 AROUND TOWN

READING

1 **Look at the photos. In which one can you see these things?**

1 a **harbour** full of boats

2 a **castle** made of ice

3 a really tall **skyscraper**

2 **SPEAKING** **Work in pairs. Name more places in a town.**

station, shop, museum

3 **SPEAKING** **How important are these buildings for a town? Think about who each building is important for and why. Compare your ideas with another pair.**

> *A hotel is important for tourists. They need a place to stay.*

4 **Work in pairs. Discuss the questions.**

1 What is the **population** of your town?

2 Does your town have a **festival** each year?

5 🔊 **2.25** **Read and listen to the blogs. Answer the questions.**

1 Where are the writers living now?

2 Where are they going to live?

3 When are they moving?

6 **Are the sentences 'Right' (A) or 'Wrong' (B)? If there is not enough information to answer 'Right' (A) or 'Wrong' (B), choose 'Doesn't say' (C).**

1 Alice's mum's job is for a year and a half.

  A Right   B Wrong   C Doesn't say

2 Alice is worried about getting bored in Dubai.

  A Right   B Wrong   C Doesn't say

3 She is excited by the Arab culture.

  A Right   B Wrong   C Doesn't say

4 It gets very cold in Yellowknife.

  A Right   B Wrong   C Doesn't say

5 The Snowking Winter Festival takes place on ice.

  A Right   B Wrong   C Doesn't say

6 Brian really likes sport.

  A Right   B Wrong   C Doesn't say

Alice's World

Today – rain in London. Tomorrow – sun in Dubai! It's time to go. We're going to fly out tomorrow! I am soooo excited! OK, I'm a bit sad to say goodbye to my friends but we aren't going to be in Dubai too long. Mum's contract is only for 18 months. Actually, that's quite a long time but I'm certainly not going to get bored. There are loads of things to do in Dubai. Here's what I'm going to do:

- Go to the top of the Burj al Arab (you know – that building that looks like a ship's sail).
- Visit Port Jebel Ali – the largest man-made harbour in the world.
- Shop – there are zillions of shopping malls there. You can go skiing in one of them.
- Eat Middle Eastern food – I just love it.
- Get into khaliji music – it's amazing.
- Play some golf in the desert (yes, it's possible), and see some tennis at the Dubai tennis stadium.
- And go to school, of course. I'm going to go to the Dubai British School.

I think that's enough to keep me busy!

■ THiNK VALUES ■

Appreciating other cultures

1 Read and tick (✓) the things you do.

You are on an exchange trip in a new country for two weeks. Which of these things would you do?

- [ ] Make friends with the local children.
- [ ] Try and find children from your own country who are also on holiday there.
- [ ] Try and learn some of the language.
- [ ] Speak your own language (and hope people understand you).
- [ ] See if the TV shows programmes from your own country.
- [ ] Read the books you brought from home.
- [ ] Visit the museums.
- [ ] Listen to and buy some music by musicians in that country.

The Life of Brian

Big news this week. We're moving! That's right, two months from now it's 'Goodbye Toronto' and 'Hello Yellowknife!'

For those of you who don't know, Yellowknife (population about 19,000) is right at the top of Canada so obviously it's pretty cold – minus 27°C in January! But it gets up to 17°C in the summer.

We're going because Dad's got a new job. He's going to work for a diamond company there.

Anyway the best thing about Yellowknife is every winter there's this really cool festival. It's called the Snowking Winter Festival. Basically, every year they build a really big ice castle on the frozen lake. Then they have loads of concerts and activities for children. They even show films on the walls of the castle. I'm definitely going to that. It's also a really good place to see the Northern Lights. I promise to take loads of photos and put them on my blog.

My sister and I are going to study at the Sir John Franklin High School. It's got a really good theatre so I'm going to do some acting there for sure. There's also a good sports centre too. It's going to be different but I'm sure I'm going to have a good time. And don't worry – I'm not going to stop writing my blog.

2 **SPEAKING** **Work in pairs. Decide which of the things in Exercise 1 are good to help you find out more about a different culture. What other things can you think of that are also good to do?**

GRAMMAR
be going to for intentions

1 Complete the sentences from the blogs on page 93 with the correct form of the verb *be*. Use contractions when you can. Then circle the correct words to complete the rule.

0 I _'m_ going to do some acting there for sure.
1 He _____ going to work for a diamond company.
2 We _____ going to be in Dubai too long.
3 My sister and I _____ going to study at the High School.
4 I _____ not going to stop writing my blog.

> **RULE:** Use *be going to* to talk about our intentions for the [1]*future / present*.
> Use the present tense of *be + going to* + [2]*base form / -ing form* of the verb.

2 Complete the table.

Positive	Negative	Questions	Short answers
I'm (am) going to play	I'm not (am not) going to play	Am I going to play?	Yes, [5]_____ . No, I'm not.
you/we/they're (are) going to play	you/we/they [1]_____ (are not) going to play	[3]_____ you/we/they going to play?	Yes, you/we/they [6]_____ . No, you/we/they aren't.
he/she/it's (is) going to play	he/she/it [2]_____ (is not) going to play	[4]_____ he/she/it going to play?	Yes, he/she/it is. No, he/she/it [7]_____ .

3 Complete the future intentions with the correct form of the verbs in the list.

~~not watch~~ | take | not fight | not borrow | do | eat

Some family plans – to make us happier!

0 I _'m not going to watch_ so much TV.
1 My parents _____ out more often.
2 We _____ all _____ more exercise.
3 My brother _____ with me anymore.
4 I _____ the dog for a walk every day.
5 My sisters _____ my clothes without asking any more.

4 Look at the table. Tick (✓) the things you are going to do.

tonight	this week	this year
do homework	play sport	write a blog
watch TV	visit relatives	have a holiday
tidy your room	play a computer game	learn something new

5 **SPEAKING** Work in pairs. Ask and answer questions about the activities in Exercise 4.

> Are you going to watch TV tonight?

> Yes, I am.

> What are you going to watch?

Workbook page 90

VOCABULARY
Places in a town

1 Match the places in the town with the people. Write 1–8 in the boxes.

1 concert hall | 2 car park
3 shopping mall | 4 bus station
5 police station | 6 post office
7 football stadium | 8 sports centre

2 **SPEAKING** Work in pairs. Describe a place from Exercise 1 for your partner to guess.

> You go here to buy clothes.

Workbook page 92

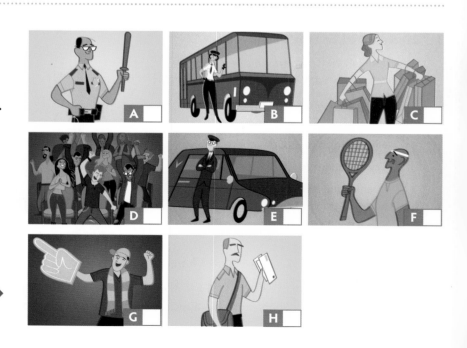

LISTENING

1 🔊2.26 **Listen to Tom and Annie. Who is Tom going to the cinema with: Emily or Annie?**

2 🔊2.26 **Listen again and complete the sentences with places in a town.**

1 Tom wants to take Annie to the _____ .
2 There's a new _____ in Bridge Street.
3 The restaurant is next to the _____ .
4 Annie is meeting Emily at the _____ .
5 Annie's relatives want to see the _____ .

GRAMMAR
Present continuous for arrangements

1 **Look at the examples. Circle the correct options. Then complete the rule with the words in the list.**

1 What *are you doing / do you do* tonight?
2 I'*m having / have* dinner with my dad. We'*re going / go* to a restaurant.

present | future | arrangements

> **RULE:** We can use the [1]_____ continuous to talk about [2]_____ for the [3]_____ .

2 **Complete the sentences. Use the present continuous form of the verb.**

0 I *'m going* (go) to Dan's party on Saturday.
1 Oliver _____ (not come) to my house this afternoon.
2 Sara and I _____ (do) our homework together after school.
3 We _____ (not visit) my grandparents on Sunday.
4 _____ your class _____ (go) on a trip next week?
5 My brother _____ (play) in the basketball final on Monday.

3 **Complete the conversation. Use the present continuous form of the verbs in the list.**

not do (x2) | go | buy | meet | do (x2) | play

KENNY   What [1]_____ you _____ this afternoon?
OLIVIA   Nothing. I [2]_____ anything.
KENNY   Paul and I [3]_____ football. Do you want to come?
OLIVIA   OK. Can I invite Tim? He [4]_____ anything either.
KENNY   Sure. And what about your brother? [5]_____ he _____ anything?
OLIVIA   Yes, he [6]_____ shopping with my mum. They [7]_____ his birthday present.
KENNY   OK. Well, we [8]_____ Jack, Adam, Lucy and Julia at the park at two.
OLIVIA   OK. See you at two, then.   **Workbook page 90** ▶

3 🔊2.26 **Listen again and complete Annie's diary.**

FRIDAY: *dinner with Dad*
SATURDAY: 1 _____
           2 _____
SUNDAY: 3 _____

FUNCTIONS
Inviting and making arrangements

1 **Complete the sentences.**

Inviting	[1]_____ _____ like to go the cinema with me? [2]_____ _____ want to go to the cinema with me?
Accepting	I'd [3]_____ to. That would be great.
Refusing	I'm sorry. I [4]_____ . I'm busy.

2 **Work in pairs. Take turns to invite your partner to do these things.**

watch DVD | go theatre | play tennis
go burger bar | come your house

3 **Think of three arrangements and write them in your diary.**

Saturday	Sunday
morning:	morning:
afternoon:	afternoon:

4 **Can you complete your diary? Walk around the classroom and:**

1 invite people to do things with you.
2 find things to do when you're free.

> *Would you like to go to a football match with me on Saturday afternoon?*

> *I'd love to.*

READING

1. Look at the photos. What problem does each one show?

2. Read the letters page and match the problems with the photos. Write 1–4 in the boxes.

A

B

C

D

Our Town:
What's wrong and what can we do about it?

1 Our town looks a mess and that's not good for tourism. I hate the litter in our streets. Why can't people put it in the bins? It's not difficult. We need to educate people quickly. We need more litter bins and billboards saying 'Don't drop it – Bin it!' and things like that.

We also need to punish people who drop litter. I think they should spend a day picking it up.
Charlie, 14

2 People always complain about the kids in our town. They don't like us hanging out in the shopping centre. They say they don't feel safe. But they're wrong. We never cause trouble. We only meet up there because there's nowhere for us to go. It's not easy being a kid. We need more things for young people to do and more places for us to go. A youth club would be great. There are lots of empty buildings in our town centre. They could use one of them.
Mack, 15

3 The biggest problem in our town is the cars. There are too many cars on our roads and the drivers don't care about the pedestrians. They drive really fast. Some of them don't even stop at zebra crossings! I ride my bike everywhere and I just don't feel very safe, even when I'm in a cycle lane. We can stop this problem easily. Let's get more speed cameras to catch these fast drivers and then stop them from driving in our town.
Pauline, 15

4 People like to complain about the graffiti on the shops in the high street. They think it's ugly. I agree that a lot of it is. But if you look closely some of this art is really good. Some of these people paint really well. Why don't we use them to make the town more attractive? I think we should create graffiti walls where these artists can show off their art. Maybe this will stop the problem of them doing it illegally.
Paris, 13

3. Read the letters page again. Answer the questions.

1. What does Charlie think people who drop litter should do?
2. What does Mack think young people need in the town?
3. What does Pauline want to stop?
4. What does Paris think will help stop the graffiti problem?

▮TRAIN TO THiNK ▮
Problem solving

1 **SPEAKING** Work in pairs. Read and discuss the problem.

The young people in your town aren't happy. They say there is nothing to do.

Make a list of suggestions to help solve this problem.

have a music festival
build a skateboard park

2 Think about your suggestions. What are the advantages and disadvantages of each one?

Suggestions	😊	☹️
music festival	*young people love music / fun*	*noisy / make a mess / expensive*

3 **SPEAKING** Decide which suggestion you think is the best. Compare your ideas with the rest of the class.

> *We think a musical festival is the best idea because all young people love music. It's also a lot of fun.*

GRAMMAR
Adverbs

1 Look at the sentences from the letters page on page 96. <u>Underline</u> the adjectives and (circle) the adverbs.

0 They drive really (fast.)

1 We can stop this problem easily.

2 It's not easy being young.

3 Let's get more speed cameras to catch these fast drivers.

4 We need to educate people quickly.

5 Some of this art is really good.

6 Some of these people paint really well.

2 Complete the rule.

> **RULE:** To form adverbs:
> - add ¹_____ to regular adjectives (e.g. *quick → quickly*).
> - delete the 'y' and add ²_____ to adjectives ending in -y.
>
> Some adjectives have irregular adverb forms.
> e.g. *fast → fast   good →* ³_____
>
> Adverbs usually come immediately after the object of the verb or the verb (if there is no object). *He plays tennis well.* NOT *He plays well tennis.*

3 Complete the sentences. Choose the correct words and write them in the correct form.

0 His car was really ___*fast*___ . He won the race ___*easily*___ . (easy / fast)

1 Her French is very _____ . She speaks really _____ . (good / fluent)

2 It's not _____ . You need to do it very _____ . (careful / easy)

3 We need to walk _____ . I don't want to be _____ . (late / quick)

4 I did my homework _____ . I was really _____ . (tired / bad)

5 He drives really _____ . I get quite _____ in the car with him. (scared / dangerous)

Workbook page 91

VOCABULARY
Things in town: compound nouns

1 Choose a word from A and a word from B to make things you can find in a town. Look at the letters on page 96 to help you.

A zebra | youth | speed | graffiti cycle | litter | bill | high

B wall | street | camera | bin | lane | crossing | board | club

2 Complete the sentences with the words in Exercise 1.

0 Slow down. There's a ___*speed camera*___ just ahead.

1 I really like that _____ advertising the new Italian restaurant in town.

2 Don't drop your paper on the floor. There's a _____ behind you.

3 Don't try and cross the road here – there's a _____ just down there.

4 We live in a flat above one of the shops in the _____ .

5 The new _____ is really popular. Loads of people are painting on it.

6 I ride my bike to school. There's a _____ from outside my house all the way there.

7 We go to the _____ every Friday night. I usually play table tennis and chat with my friends there.

Workbook page 92

Pronunciation
Voiced /ð/ and unvoiced /θ/ consonants

Go to page 121.

Culture

1 Look at the photos. What do you think a ghost town is?

2 Read the article quickly. Where are these towns?

3 🔊2.29 Read the article again and listen. Mark the sentences T (true) or F (false).

1 Kolmanskop was once a very rich town.
2 The UFO buildings are a popular tourist attraction in Taipei.
3 Fordlândia became a problem because there was nowhere for the factory workers to live.
4 The Ford family sold Fordlândia for $20 million.
5 They closed Centralia because of an accident.
6 It still isn't safe to visit Centralia today.

Ghost Towns around the World

We build towns for people to live in. But what happens when they don't want to live in them any longer? All over the world there are ghost towns, towns where people don't live any more. Here are a few.

In 1908, many Germans arrived in Luderitz in the southern African country of Namibia. They wanted to look for diamonds and they found a lot. With the money from the diamonds they built the town of Kolmanskop. It had lots of beautiful buildings, a hospital, a school, and even a theatre. But when there weren't any more diamonds, they left the town. These days the only things that visitors to Kolmanskop see are empty buildings and a lot of sand.

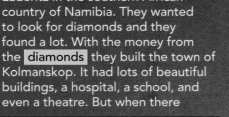

In 1978, a building company started building a holiday resort in the Sanzhi District of New Taipei City. For the next two years they built a lot of round buildings. They didn't look like normal houses, but more like spaceships. People called them the 'UFO houses'. In 1980, they stopped building the houses because there wasn't enough money and for 28 years the resort was a ghost town. However, no one can visit this city today because in 2008 they demolished all the buildings. All we can see now are photos of these strange looking houses.

In Northern Brazil, there is the ghost town of Fordlândia. In 1928, Henry Ford – famous for his cars – decided to build a big factory there to make car tyres. He also built houses for the workers and their families. Unfortunately, the weather in the area wasn't good for growing the trees they needed to

make tyres. Ford tried to make the city a success but it was difficult. In 1945, his grandson Henry Ford II sold Fordlândia. The company lost $20 million. The empty buildings of the town are still there today.

About 70 years ago, Centralia was a busy town in Pennsylvania, USA. It had five hotels, seven churches and 19 big stores. In 1962, a fire started under the town at an old mine. They spent millions of dollars trying to stop it but that didn't work. It became too dangerous to live there and everyone had to leave the town. These days a sign across the road to the town tells people to 'stay out'. The fire is still burning today.

4 VOCABULARY **There are six highlighted words in the article. Match the words with these meanings. Write the words.**

0	very expensive stones	*diamonds*
1	destroyed	
2	a company that makes houses	
3	a small holiday village or town	
4	you find a lot of it on beaches and in the desert	
5	holes in the ground from where substances such as coal, metal and salt are removed	

5 SPEAKING **Work in pairs. Discuss.**

1 Imagine you are going to make a film set in one of these towns. Think about:
- What kind of film is it? (horror, love, science fiction?)
- What's the story about briefly? (It's about a ...)
- Who is going to star in your film? (It's going to star my favourite actors ...)

2 Present your ideas to the group and vote on the best idea.

WRITING
An informal email

1 **Read the email. Answer the questions.**

1 Where is Emily going to spend her summer holidays?

2 What is she going to do there?

2 **Find these expressions in the email. Use them to answer the questions below.**

Guess what? | You won't believe it. | I can't wait.
By the way, ... | Anyway, ...

1 Which two expressions do we use to change topic?

2 Which two expressions do we use to introduce some surprising news?

3 Which expression means 'I'm really excited'?

3 **Look at paragraphs 1 and 2 of Emily's email. Match the functions with the paragraphs. Write a–d.**

Paragraph 1: _____ and _____
Paragraph 2: _____ and _____

a Describe the city b Give news
c Ask how your friend is d Talk about your plans

4 **What is the function of paragraph 3?**

5 **Which paragraph answers these questions?**

a What famous buildings are there in Sydney?
b What's your news?
c How long are you going to stay in Sydney?
d What's the weather like in Sydney?
e What are you going to do in Sydney?
f Where are you going?

6 **Imagine you are going to spend your next holiday in a famous city. Write an email (about 100–120 words) to your friend telling her the news.**

- Use the questions in Exercise 5 to help you.
- Use some of the language in Exercise 2.

To: luckyluke@writeme.co.uk
Subject: Exciting news!

Hi Luke,

[1] How are you? I hope you're not studying too hard. Don't worry, there are only two more weeks of school. Anyway, I'm writing because I've got some really cool news. You won't believe it. Mum and Dad are taking me to Sydney for the summer. Sydney, Australia! I can't wait.

[2] So I did some research on the Internet. It looks like a really amazing place. Of course, there's the famous harbour with the bridge and the Opera House but there are so many other great things to do there. I'm definitely going to hang out on Bondi Beach. And guess what? Mum's going to buy me some surfing lessons. I'm going to be a surfer! We're going to be there for the whole of August. It's winter there but I think the Australian winter is hotter than our summer. So that's it – my big news. What do you think?

[3] By the way, Dad says we're going to be in Bangor next weekend. Is there any chance we can meet up? Let me know.

Love

Emily

CAMBRIDGE ENGLISH: Key

■ THiNK EXAMS

READING AND WRITING

Part 2: Multiple-choice sentence completion Workbook page 61

1 **Read the sentences about holiday plans. Choose the best word (A, B or C) for each space.**

0 On Monday we're _____ to Rio de Janeiro.
   A to fly   Ⓑ flying   C fly

1 It's one of the _____ beautiful cities in the world.
   A most   B more   C less

2 The weather there is lovely. It's usually hot and very _____ .
   A freezing   B foggy   C sunny

3 We're _____ to visit my uncle and his family in Brazil.
   A going   B go   C to go

4 I'm also a bit scared because I _____ speak Portuguese.
   A can   B not   C can't

5 Mum says I shouldn't worry, because my cousins all speak English very _____ .
   A well   B good   C badly

Part 7: Open cloze Workbook page 89

2 **Complete the text about Llandudno. Write ONE word for each space.**

LISTENING

Part 5: Note completion Workbook page 79

3 🔊2.30 **You will hear some information about a shopping centre. Listen and complete each question.**

- There are over (0) ___300___ shops.
- There are restaurants and a (1) _____ on the fifth floor.
- Parking costs (2) £_____ every hour.
- Buses leave for the city centre every (3) _____ .
- Shops close at 5.30 pm every day except (4) _____ .

My name (0) ___is___ Hugo and I would like to tell you about the town where I live. It's (1) _____ the north of Wales and it's called Llandudno. That's probably (2) _____ unusual name for you, because it's a Welsh name. Here in Wales, we have our own language. I (3) _____ born here and so I speak Welsh really (4) _____ .

Llandudno is (5) _____ most beautiful town in Wales. Well, that's what I think. It's by the sea and we have lots of beaches. They're (6) _____ sandy but have lots (7) _____ small stones on them. You (8) _____ swim in the sea if you want to, but it's quite cold most of the year.

There are lots of things to do in Llandudno. There (9) _____ parks and there's a small mountain where you can take a chair lift to a café at the top. There's a really good concert hall and lots of great bands play here. There's (10) _____ a youth club that I go to every Friday night with my friends.

TEST YOURSELF

UNITS 9 & 10

VOCABULARY

1 Complete the sentences with the words in the list. There are two extra words.

windy | zebra | lake | hall | mountains | bin | island | lanes | cloudy | sunny | station | house

1 It's very _____ today. You can't see the sun at all.
2 We live on a small _____ . There is sea all around us.
3 Mum and Dad are going to the concert _____ tonight. They're very excited.
4 It's one of the highest _____ in the world and it took the climbers three days to get to the top.
5 It's so _____ that my hat just blew off my head.
6 Don't try and cross the road here. There's a _____ crossing just up there.
7 It's easy to get about town on a bike because there are cycle _____ everywhere.
8 I lost my wallet in the city centre. I went to the police _____ but they didn't have it.
9 Put your rubbish in the litter _____ over there.
10 We went fishing on the _____ but we didn't catch anything.

/10

GRAMMAR

2 Put the words in order to make sentences.

1 going / She's / nine / to / me / at / phone
2 Monday / We're / morning / on / leaving
3 homework / carefully / her / did / very / She
4 keys / I / I / remember / my / where / can't / left
5 the / It's / day / hottest / of / year / the
6 than / It's / mine / car / expensive / a / more

3 Find and correct the mistake in each sentence.

1 I speak badly French.
2 This is the more popular sport in the world; everybody likes it.
3 I had a lot of presents. But the one most I liked was a blue watch from my mother.
4 She plays tennis very good.
5 He's ten and he still can't to ride a bike.
6 We are to meeting him at nine o'clock.

/12

FUNCTIONAL LANGUAGE

4 Write the missing words.

1 A _____ a horrible day!
  B Yes, _____ stay inside and watch TV.
2 A What are you _____ later?
  B Nothing. Why?
  A _____ you want to go skateboarding with me?
3 A _____ you like to come to my house for dinner on Friday?
  B I'd _____ to. Thanks.
4 A _____ what?
  B What?
  A Mum's taking me to Disneyland Paris this summer. I _____ wait!

/8

MY SCORE /30

| 22 – 30 |
| 10 – 21 |
| 0 – 9 |

READING

1 Label the picture with the words in the list. Write 1–12 in the boxes.

1 arm | 2 leg | 3 mouth | 4 muscle | 5 finger | 6 foot
7 ear | 8 eye | 9 toe | 10 hair | 11 bone | 12 thumb

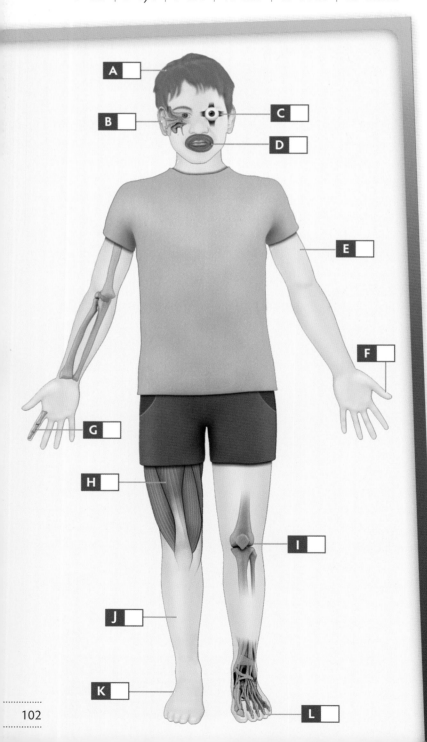

2 Write the words from Exercise 1 in the correct column.

Body	Face
arm	*mouth*

3 **SPEAKING** Work in pairs. Discuss the questions.

Which parts of the body do you use when you:

- read a book?
- play football?
- watch television?
- make a phone call?
- eat a meal?
- walk to school?

> *When you read a book you use your hands and your eyes.*

4 Look at the picture on page 103 and the title. What do you think the article will be about? Choose one of the following.

1 What we want to look like in the future.
2 What the human body will be like in the future.
3 How we can change our bodies if we want.

5 ◀ᴅ)) **2.31** Read and listen to the article and check your ideas.

6 Read the article again and answer the questions.

1 What is the most important reason why our bodies will change in the future?
2 Why will people be taller?
3 Why will people get weaker?
4 What will happen to eyes and fingers?
5 Why will we have one less toe?
6 Why won't people have so much hair on their bodies?

Changing bodies

A long time ago, people were very different from the way we are now. For example, if you find a really old house somewhere, you'll see that the doors are usually much lower than they are today. Why? Because hundreds of years ago, people were shorter. Over time, the human body changes to adapt to a new way of life.

Can we expect the human body to change in the future? For sure. And the main reason is that we have more and more technology, and it is changing how we live.

What kind of changes can we expect? Well, no one can be 100 per cent sure, but here are some possibilities.

1 Let's start with the example above. Humans are now ten centimetres taller than 150 years ago. So, in the future, people will probably be even taller. Most of us now have much better food than people in the past – and so we grow more.

2 We'll get weaker in more than one way. The most important way is that our muscles will not be as strong as now because we won't do a lot of physical work.

3 We are already using our feet less, and our hands more (think about computers and tablets and so on.) So we can expect that our legs will get shorter and our feet smaller, and at the same time, our fingers will get longer. And our fingers and our eyes will both get better, because they'll have to do more work together.

4 Now, what about the mouth? It'll get smaller, perhaps, because technological improvements will mean that we don't need to talk so much – and also because our teeth will get smaller (so mouths don't need to be so big to keep them in).

5 Here's a good one – it's very possible that people will have four toes, not five. The little toe really isn't needed any more (people who lose them don't miss them) so it will probably disappear some time in the future.

6 And last but not least – people won't have as much hair on their bodies as now, as we don't need it to keep ourselves warm any more.

Will all these things happen? And if so, when? These are questions that no one can answer for sure.

■ THiNK VALUES ■

Exercise and health

1 **Read the sentences. Give each one a number from 1 to 5 (1 = doesn't give a lot of importance to health and 5 = gives a lot of importance to health).**

1 ☐ You should do regular exercise to make sure your muscles are strong.

2 ☐ It's OK to spend a lot of time sitting in front of the television.

3 ☐ A wonderful thing to do is go for long walks in the fresh air.

4 ☐ Using a computer and writing text messages gives your hands and arms exercise.

5 ☐ You don't have to do sport to be healthy and keep fit.

6 ☐ It's a good idea to do a lot of simple exercise (for example, use the stairs and don't take the lift).

2 **SPEAKING Work in small groups. Talk about health and exercise.**

1 Together, decide the number that the group is going to give to each of the sentences in Exercise 1.

2 Together, decide on and write another sentence that shows how the group feels about health and exercise.

3 Compare your ideas with other groups.

GRAMMAR
will / won't for future predictions

1 Look at the sentences from the article on page 103. Complete with *will / 'll / won't*. Then complete the rule.

1 Our fingers _____ get longer.

2 They _____ have to do more work together.

3 Our muscles _____ be as strong as now, because we _____ do a lot of physical work.

> **RULE:** Use ¹_____ (*will*) or ²_____ (*will not*) + base form of the verb to make predictions about the future.

2 Complete the table.

Positive	Negative
I/you/we/they/he/she/it ¹_____ (will) come	I/you/we/they/he/she/it ²_____ (will not) come

Questions	Short answers
³_____ I/you/we/they/he/she/it come?	Yes, I/you/we/they/he/she/it ⁴_____ . No, I/you/we/they/he/she/it ⁵_____ (will not).

3 Complete the conversation. Use *'ll, will* or *won't* and a verb from the list.

~~get~~ | stay | go | see | give | be | help

ALICE Oh, Mark, it's the French test tomorrow! I hate French. I'm sure I ⁰ ___*won't get*___ the answers right!

MARK Don't worry, you ¹_____ fine! You got a good result in your last test.

ALICE Yes, but this is more difficult. I really don't feel well. Maybe I ²_____ to school tomorrow. I ³_____ in bed all day.

MARK That ⁴_____ you. The teacher ⁵_____ you the test on Wednesday.

ALICE You're right. But what can I do?

MARK Look, why don't I come round to your place this afternoon after school? We can do some French together. You ⁶_____ that it's not so difficult.

ALICE Oh, thanks, Mark.

4 **SPEAKING** Work in pairs. Act out the conversation in Exercise 3.

Workbook page 100

> ## Pronunciation
> The /h/ consonant sound
> **Go to page 121.**

VOCABULARY
Parts of the body

1 Match the words with the photos. Write numbers 1–10 in the boxes.

1 ankle | 2 back | 3 elbow | 4 knees | 5 lips | 6 neck | 7 shoulder | 8 stomach | 9 throat | 10 tongue

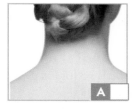
A

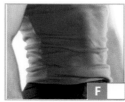
F

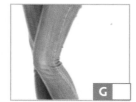
B

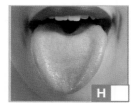
G

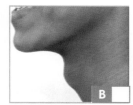
C

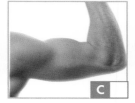
H

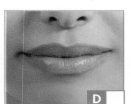
D

I

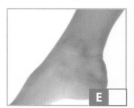
E

J

2 **2.34** Listen and match the speakers (1, 2 and 3) with the pictures. Write numbers 1–3 in the boxes.

A

B

C

Workbook page 102

LISTENING

1 Look at the pictures A–C. Answer these questions for each one.

1 Who are the two people?
2 Where are the two people?

2 🔊2.35 Listen to three conversations. Match the pictures with the conversations. Complete the table. Write A, B or C in the 'Speakers' column and D, E or F in the 'Problem' column.

	Speakers (A, B, or C)	Problem (D, E, or F)
Conversation 1		
Conversation 2		
Conversation 3		

3 🔊2.35 Listen again. Mark the statements T (true) or F (false).

1 Katie hurt her shoulder while she was watching skateboarding.
2 When Katie fell, it wasn't a bad fall.
3 David's ankle hurts all the time.
4 David's mother wants to take him to the doctor.
5 Sam didn't tell his parents about his back.
6 Molly wants to take Sam to see the doctor at school.

4 Who said these things? Match the sentences with the speakers.

1 Are you all right?   a the doctor
2 Does it hurt?   b David's mother
3 What's the matter?   c Sam
4 It hurts a bit.   d Molly
5 My shoulder hurts.   e David
6 I've got backache.   f Katie

SPEAKING

Work in pairs. Choose one of the pictures above (A, B or C) in Exercise 2. Role play the conversation.

1 Decide who will be each person in the picture.
2 Choose a different part of the body from the conversation you heard for your picture (example: for Picture A, choose 'head' not 'back').
3 Have a conversation.
4 Now choose another picture. Change roles.

■ THiNK SELF-ESTEEM ■

Getting help

1 Read and tick (✓) the sentences that are true for you.

1 ☐ I don't like going to the doctor and so I don't go.
2 ☐ If I have a problem, I don't like telling other people about it.
3 ☐ If I don't feel well, I tell someone.
4 ☐ I don't want other people to worry about me.
5 ☐ It's OK to get help from people around you.
6 ☐ It's important to go to the doctor if you often have the same health problem.

2 SPEAKING Compare your ideas in class.

3 Who can you talk to about these problems?

1 a headache   3 difficult homework
2 a problem at school 4 a problem with a friend

LOOK!

stomach ache

ear ache

headache

toothache

READING

1 Read the webchats. Write a name under each picture: Arlene, Pete, Susie, Julia or Mike.

2 Read the webchats again. Who talks about these things? Write the names.

1 eyes _____
2 a vegetable _____
3 dangerous things _____
4 making faces _____
5 making a noise _____

3 **SPEAKING** Do you know any more 'crazy' things that adults say to children? Tell the class.

A _____

B _____

C _____

D _____

E _____

Crazy things that parents say to their kids ✕

Arlene
Now I'm eighteen, I can look back at all those happy days when I was a kid at home! And I remember the things that my mum and dad said to me again and again. For example: when my sister and I were making a noise, my father always said, 'If I have to come over there, you won't be happy to see me!' lol. Did your parents ever say things like that to you?

👍 **LIKE · COMMENT · SHARE**

Pete
Oh of course! My little brother and me, we loved TV and we sat and watched it for hours every day. And my mum always looked at us and said, 'If you watch TV all the time, you'll get square eyes.' Well, we watched a lot of TV and our eyes are still normal. haha!

Susie
You reminded me, Pete. My dad always said, 'If you sit too close to the TV, you'll go blind.' But he had another favourite too (I think he was always worried about our eyes, for some reason) – he said, 'If you eat all your carrots, you'll see in the dark.' I really like carrots – I ate them when I was a kid and I eat them now – but I still can't see in the dark!

Julia
I always liked doing dangerous things – you know, climbing trees and things. And my dad said, 'If you fall you'll break your leg.' And he always added, 'And when you break your leg, don't come running to me for help!' I didn't understand the joke for years!

Mike
Nice one, Julia! OK here's another one, and I think every child in the world hears this. If I was angry or upset, I always made a face, and my mum said, 'If you go on making that face, the wind will change and your face will stay like that forever!' That's the only one I remember – but as soon as I think of others, I'll send them to you!

GRAMMAR
First conditional

1 Match the parts of the sentences. Check your answers in the webchats. Then complete the rule and the table. Choose the correct words.

1 ☐ If you eat all your carrots,
2 ☐ If I have to come over there,
3 ☐ If you fall,

a you won't be happy to see me.
b you'll break your leg.
c you'll see in the dark.

RULE: Use the first conditional to talk about [1]*possible / certain* events and their [2]*present / future* results.

If clause	Result clause
If + present simple,	[3]_____ ('ll) [4]_____ (won't) + base form

It is possible to put the result clause first:
If you fall, you'll hurt yourself. OR
You'll hurt yourself if you fall.

2 Put the words in order to make sentences.

0 see Jane, / If / tell / I / I'll / her
   If I see Jane, I'll tell her.

1 my parents / I'm / will / If / late, / be angry

2 I / bring it / I'll / to school tomorrow / If / remember,

3 you'll / Jake / come / If / you / meet / to the party,

4 rain tomorrow / if / the / it / doesn't / We'll / to / beach / go

5 the concert / if / tonight / I / don't / I / won't / feel better / go / to

3 Complete the first conditional sentences with the correct form of the verbs.

0 If Kate ___gives___ (give) me some help, I _'ll finish_ (finish) my homework in an hour.

1 You _____ (not meet) anyone if you _____ (not go out).

2 I _____ (come) to your party if my mum _____ (say) I can.

3 If Ken _____ (not want) his ice cream, I _____ (eat) it.

4 Susan _____ (be) angry if she _____ (hear) about this.

5 If we _____ (buy) hamburgers, we _____ (not have) enough money for the film.

ROLE PLAY

Work in pairs. Student A: Go to page 127. Student B: Go to page 128. Ask and answer the questions.

Workbook page 101

Time clauses with *when / as soon as*

4 Read the two sentences and answer the questions. Then complete the rule with *will* and *present simple*.

When we get to school, I'll take you to see the nurse.

As soon as I think of other examples, I'll tell you.

1 What is the difference between *when* and *as soon as*?

2 Do *get* and *think* refer to the present or future?

RULE: In sentences about the future, we use the 1_____ form after *if* or *when* or *as soon as*, and 2_____ + base form of the verb in the main clause.

5 Complete the sentences. Use the verbs in the list.

finish (x2) | get (x2) | arrive

1 As soon as I _____ my exam results, I'll phone you.

2 When I _____ home, I'll check my messages.

3 The party will start as soon as my friend _____ with the music!

4 When the game _____ we'll go and have a pizza.

5 I'll lend you the book as soon as I _____ reading it.

Workbook page 101

VOCABULARY
when and *if*

1 Match sentences 1 and 2 with the explanations.

1 **When I see Martin**, I'll give him your message.

2 **If I see Martin**, I'll give him your message.

a It is possible that I will meet Martin.

b I know that I will meet Martin.

2 Complete the sentences with *if* or *when*.

0 I can't talk to you now. I'll phone you _when_ I get home.

1 A What are you doing tomorrow?
   B _____ there's a good film on, I'll probably go to the cinema.

2 I'm not sure if I want to go to the party tonight. But _____ I decide to go, I'll phone you.

3 It's too hot to go for a walk now. Let's go out in the evening, _____ it's cooler.

4 You can watch some TV _____ you finish your homework, and not before!

5 It's the football final tonight. I'll be very happy _____ my team wins.

Workbook page 102

LISTENING AND WRITING
A phone message

1 Which of these things do you NOT need to write down if you take a phone message? Mark the things with a cross (✗).

1 the name of the caller ☐

2 the telephone number of the person who takes the message ☐

3 the name of the person who the message is for ☐

4 the telephone number of the caller ☐

5 what the caller wants ☐

2 ◁))2.36 Listen to a telephone conversation. Complete the message.

Message from: ¹_____
For: ²_____
Message: *she needs* ³_____ .
Please ⁴_____
Number to call: ⁵_____

107

The phone call

1 ◀))2.37 **Read and listen to the photostory and answer the questions.**

Why is Megan's father stressed?

Who phones Megan while she's in the park?

OLIVIA Aw, look!

LUKE Looks like they're having a good time.

WOMAN Jason?! You stop that. Do you hear me? Stop it!

RYAN What did you say, Luke?

OLIVIA Well, we all know what that's like – your parents, shouting at you.

1

MEGAN Oh, don't, please! The last couple of days …

RYAN What?

MEGAN Oh, my dad. He's really stressed. He's got a big business meeting he has to attend, out of town tomorrow and Friday.

LUKE Something important?

2

MEGAN I suppose so. I don't know.

RYAN Well, I think you *should* know. I mean, he's your father, right? Family and stuff.

MEGAN Yeah, yeah. Whatever. But I know one thing: he shouts at me all the time. Everything I do is wrong.

OLIVIA Poor you.

WOMAN Jason! I told you – don't do that! If I have to go over there …

MEGAN Just like that. Another few years and I can leave home! I can't wait!

3

OLIVIA Just think, Megan. You'll be a mother too one day. Then you'll remember this.

RYAN That's right. And when we're parents, we'll be just the same as our parents. Wait and see.

MEGAN Hello? Oh, hello, Dad. What is it? I'm in the park.

LUKE Tell you what, though. If our parents weren't …

MEGAN Shh!! Dad, say that again. What? The hospital? Mum?

4

DEVELOPING SPEAKING

2 Work in pairs. Discuss what happens next in the story. Write down your ideas.

Perhaps Megan has to go to the hospital.

3 ◼◄ **EP6** Watch to find out how the story continues.

4 Answer the questions.

1 What happened to Megan's mother?
2 When will her mother go home?
3 What is the problem for Megan's father?
4 Why can Megan help without going to school?
5 What does Megan say to the others is 'the good thing'?
6 What does Luke mean when he says: 'It's all ups and downs'?

PHRASES FOR FLUENCY

1 Find the expressions 1–6 in the story. Who says them? Match them to the definitions a–f.

1	I suppose so.	a	What I want to say is …
2	I mean, …	b	I really don't care.
3	Whatever.	c	Here's what I think …
4	I can't wait.	d	I think that's possibly true.
5	Wait and see.	e	You'll know in the future.
6	Tell you what …	f	I hope it happens very soon.

2 Complete the conversations. Use the expressions 1–6 in Exercise 1.

1 A I'm going to see the new Ryan Gosling film on Saturday! _____ !
  B _____ – we could go together. _____ , if that's OK with you.

2 A What are you going to give me for my birthday?
  B _____ . It's a surprise!

3 A You look so funny in that yelllow shirt.
  B _____ , Alex.

4 A Can I go out tonight, Dad?
  B _____ . But don't be late back, OK?

WordWise

Expressions with *do*

1 Complete the sentences from the video.

1 She was doing some _____ upstairs.
2 I can do the _____ and everything.
3 Thanks. She's doing _____ , though.

2 Complete the sentences with a word from the list.

ice cream | homework | cooking | well

1 Joe's upstairs – he's doing his _____ .
2 Did you do _____ in your exam?
3 They do great _____ at the new café.
4 Mum has a rest on Sundays and we all do the _____ .

3 **SPEAKING** Complete the questions. Then ask and answer with a partner.

1 _____ you _____ a lot of exercise?
2 Where _____ you _____ your homework?
3 _____ you _____ OK with your schoolwork these days?
4 Who _____ the cleaning in your house?

Workbook page 102 ➤

FUNCTIONS
Sympathising

1 Complete the extracts from the story with the phrases in the list.

Poor you. | That's a shame.
I'm sorry to hear that. | poor thing.

1 MEGAN But I know one thing: he shouts at me all the time. Everything I do is wrong.
  OLIVIA _____ .

2 MEGAN Oh, _____ . Well, she'll be home tomorrow.
  DAD That's right. Then a few days at home.

3 RYAN _____ , Megan.
  OLIVIA Me too.
  MEGAN Thanks. She's doing OK, though.

4 MEGAN But it means I can't go out with you guys on Friday.
  RYAN _____ .

2 Read the situations. What can you say in each one?

1 You meet a friend. You know that your friend lost something important yesterday.

> *Poor you!*

2 You hear that Alex broke his arm last weekend. You meet Alex's brother.
3 Your neighbour says: 'I feel terrible today – I think I'm ill.'

12 | TRAVELLERS' TALES

A

B

C

READING

1 Match the words with the photos. Write 1–6 in the boxes.

1 bicycle | 2 bus | 3 boat | 4 car | 5 plane | 6 train

2 Name other kinds of transport in English.

3 SPEAKING Work in pairs. Ask and answer the questions.

How do you travel …
- to school?
- to the cinema?
- to the shops?
- when you go on holiday?

> *I usually go by bike.*

> *Sometimes I take the bus. Sometimes I walk.*

> *Sometimes I walk, but sometimes my dad drives.*

4 SPEAKING Work in pairs or small groups. Read about these people. For each one, say how you think they could travel.

1 A British family – wife, husband and two children – want to go to the USA on holiday.
2 A student living in London wants to go to Paris.
3 A businesswoman who works in a city is going to a meeting on the other side of the city.
4 Three teenagers in a city want to go to a party at a house that is five kilometres away.

5 SPEAKING Think about the ways of travelling in Exercises 1 and 2. Which one(s) is (are):
- cheap?
- dangerous?
- expensive?
- boring?
- exciting?
- your favourite?
- an adventure?
- your least favourite?

E

D

F

6 Look at the photos and the title of the blog on page 111. What do you think the blog is about? Choose one of the following.

1 Someone who travels to many different places.
2 Different ways to travel.
3 Different places to travel to in the world.

7 ◀))2.38 Read and listen to the blog and check your ideas.

8 Read the blog again. Correct the information in these sentences.

1 Nora Dunn wanted to travel the world until she got old.
2 Nora gets her money from some rich friends.
3 Sometimes she writes home to ask for some money.
4 She does the same job everywhere she goes.
5 She travelled by boat to the Caribbean.
6 She has appeared on television in every country she's visited.
7 Life is always easy for her when she travels.
8 She has a website to tell people how to spend a lot of money travelling.

Ted's Travel Blog

HOME   ABOUT   NEWS   CONTACT

The non-stop traveller

Hello to all my readers. This week, I've decided to write about travel. Perhaps, like me, you've always thought that travelling is something for rich people. Well, now I think I've been wrong all this time. Why? Well, I've discovered Nora Dunn.

Nora is one of a new kind of traveller – a professional world traveller. She travels all the time. Nora is from Toronto, Canada and until she was 30, she had a business there. But then she made a big decision. Her dream was to travel the world – and to do it before she got old! So she sold her business and got rid of her belongings. And off she went.

Nora hasn't got rich parents or anyone who gives her money. And she doesn't have a high-paying job. But she's learned how to travel without spending lots of money.

Nora goes to a place and stays there for some time. She works to earn enough money to have a good time and to save a bit, then she moves on to another place. She prefers simple forms of transport like trains or buses, but of course there are times when planes are a necessity. And she writes from wherever she is, which earns her some money too. She's done a lot of different jobs, including working in hotels and in restaurants. And she's learned things like cooking and meditation.

So where has Nora been? Well, everywhere! She's been to all five continents and she's travelled to over thirty countries. All in six years! She's taken a train across Canada and she's travelled by train from Portugal to Vietnam – an incredible journey. She's lived on a boat in the Caribbean and she's worked for her accommodation in Hawaii, Australia, New Zealand, Spain, England, Grenada and Switzerland, and a number of other places too. And she's been on television shows in three countries. She's had a lot of fantastic adventures, and she hasn't stopped finding new things!

Some of her experiences have not been easy ones. In 2008 she helped people in Thailand and Burma after a cyclone hit their countries. And in 2009 she helped to fight forest fires in Australia.

So, she's seen a lot so far. She's learned that full-time travel doesn't have to be expensive, and she knows now that there are plenty of ways to do it – so many ways, in fact, that she's started a website to tell other people about them. It's theprofessionalhobo.com. I've seen lots of travel sites, and this is one of the best. Have a look. Perhaps you'll be the next 'world traveller'?

See you next week.

■ THiNK VALUES ■

Travel broadens the mind

1 **Read what people said about Nora Dunn. Match the comments 1–4 with the values a–d. Write a–d in the boxes.**

1 ☐ She's seen so many different countries, so I think she probably understands all kinds of people.

2 ☐ She's probably a better person now, because she's learned so many things.

3 ☐ I think it's wonderful, what she did in Burma with the cyclone and in Australia with the fire.

4 ☐ I think it's great that she's living her life without thinking about money all the time.

a helping other people
b self-improvement
c not worrying about money
d learning about other cultures

2 **SPEAKING** How important are the values in Exercise 1 for you? Put them in order from 1–4. Compare your ideas in class. Say why you think the values are important or not.

GRAMMAR
Present perfect simple

1 Complete the sentences from the blog on page 111. Then complete the rule.

1 Perhaps, like me, you _____ always _____ that travelling is something for rich people.

2 Now, I think I _____ wrong all this time.

3 She _____ a lot of different jobs.

4 So where _____ Nora _____ ?

5 Some of her experiences _____ easy ones.

> **RULE:** Use the present perfect to talk about actions that happened some time in your life up to now.
> Form the present perfect with the present simple form of _____ + past participle.

2 <u>Underline</u> other examples of the present perfect in the blog on page 111.

3 Complete the table.

Positive	Negative	Questions	Short answers
I/you/we/they 've (¹_____) worked	I/you/we/they haven't (have not) worked	⁴_____ I/you/we/they worked?	Yes, I/you/we/they ⁶_____ . No, I/you/we/they haven't.
he/she/it 's (²_____) worked	he/she/it hasn't (³_____) worked	⁵_____ he/she/it worked?	Yes, he/she/it has. No, he/she/it ⁷_____ .

4 Complete the past participles. Use the irregular verbs list on page 128 of the Workbook to help you.

base form	past participle	base form	past participle
0 be	_been_	6 speak	_____
1 do	_____	7 eat	_____
2 go	_____	8 take	_____
3 see	_____	9 fly	_____
4 write	_____	10 swim	_____
5 meet	_____	11 win	_____

> **LOOK!**
> 1 She **has gone** to New York. = She is not here now – she is in New York.
> 2 She **has been** to New York. = She went to New York and came back (at some time in the past).

5 Jack and Diane are 25 years old. When they were teenagers, they wanted to do many things – and they have done some of them but not all of them. Look at the table. Complete the sentences about them.

	learn French	visit Paris	write a book	work in the USA	make a lot of money
Diane	✓	✗	✓	✓	✗
Jack	✓	✓	✗	✗	✗

0 Jack and Diane _have learned_ French.

1 Diane _____ Paris.

2 Diane _____ a book.

3 Jack _____ Paris.

4 Jack _____ in the USA.

5 They _____ a lot of money.

6 **WRITING** Look at the information about Sue and Harry. Write sentences about them.

	visit another country	fly in a plane	swim in the sea	touch a snake	take a driving test
Sue	✓	✗	✗	✗	✓
Harry	✓	✓	✗	✓	✗

7 **SPEAKING** Work in pairs. Say things about yourself and people you know. Remember: don't say when in the past.

> My mother has lived in Africa.
> I've won two tennis competitions.

Workbook page 108

LISTENING

1   **◀))2.39** Steve Anderson is at his old school giving a talk about his travels. Listen to the end of Steve's talk. Mark the statements T (true) or F (false).

1   He wants to get married and start a family. ☐

2   When he was younger, he didn't like staying at home. ☐

3   He's going to stop travelling soon. ☐

2   **◀))2.40** Now the children ask Steve questions. Listen and match the events with the places.

1   ☐ The most interesting place he's been to.

2   ☐ The place where he ate a cooked spider.

3   ☐ The place where he was ill.

a   Africa   b   India   c   Mexico

3   **◀))2.40** Listen again and answer the questions.

1   Has he ever eaten snake?

2   Did he like the spider that he ate?

3   Has he had any accidents in a minibus or taxi?

4   What do tourists and travellers take with them?

GRAMMAR
Present perfect with *ever / never*

1   **Complete the sentences with *ever* or *never* and complete the rule.**

1   I've _____ eaten snake.

2   Have you _____ eaten anything really horrible?

> **RULE:** When we use the present perfect to talk about experiences and we want to say:
> - 'at no time in (my) life' we use the word [1]_____
> - 'at any time in (your) life' we use the word [2]_____
>
> The words *ever* and *never* usually come between *have* and the past participle.

2   **Complete the mini dialogues with the words in the list.**

been | yes | eaten | have
never | no | ever | played

1   A   Have you _____ watched a silent film?
    B   Yes, I _____ .

2   A   Have you ever _____ to the Olympic games?
    B   _____ , I've never been to them.

3   A   Have you ever _____ tennis?
    B   _____ , I have.

4   A   Have you ever _____ a really hot curry?
    B   No, I've _____ tried curry.

Workbook page 109 ▶

FUNCTIONS
Talking about life experiences

Work in pairs. Ask and answer the questions

1   ever / see / a snake?

2   ever / eat / something horrible?

3   ever / be / on television?

4   ever / speak / to someone from the USA?

5   ever / win / a prize?

6   ever / be / to another country?

> *Have you ever seen a snake?*

> *Yes I have. It was a python at the zoo.*

> *No, I haven't.*

SPEAKING

Work in pairs. Think of a famous person. Ask about things that the famous person has done in their life, and imagine the answers. Use some of the verbs in the list.

travel | stay | play | win | eat | see | drive | write

> *Mr President — have you ever eaten fried spiders?*

> *Yes, I have. I eat them all the time.*

■ TRAIN TO THiNK
Exploring differences

1   **SPEAKING** Work in small groups. Look at the pairs of things. Answer the questions.

a   What is the same?

b   What is different?

1   A car and a taxi

2   A train and a plane

3   A holiday and a journey

4   A tourist and a traveller

The same: a car and a taxi have wheels / doors / a driver.

Different: you drive your car but a taxi-driver drives the taxi. In a taxi, you have to pay.

2   **SPEAKING** Compare your ideas with others in the class.

> **Pronunciation**
> Sentence stress
> Go to page 121.   ◀))

READING

1 **Read the interview. Put the four questions in the correct places.**

- **a** Have you ever had any famous passengers?
- **b** Have passengers ever left anything in your taxi?
- **c** What's the worst part of your job?
- **d** When did you start?

THE TAXI DRIVER

Fiona McIntyre is a taxi driver in London. She tells us about her work and some of her experiences.

1 _____

I've been a taxi driver for about five years. Before that I was a bus driver in London, and I enjoyed it, but I wanted to be more independent so I changed and started driving my taxi.

2 _____

Oh yes. I've had film stars, politicians, you know, lots of famous people. About a year ago, a really famous actor got in my taxi. I took him to the airport. There was a lot of traffic and it took a long time to get there, so he missed his plane. It wasn't my fault but when he got out of the taxi, he said some things that weren't very polite! I said to him, 'Next time, take a bus!'

3 _____

Oh yes! People have left all kinds of things in here – a suitcase, a hat, mobile phones of course, even a dog once! Years ago, a woman left a pair of shoes on the back seat. And one time a passenger left his teeth here! Not real teeth, of course – false teeth.

And people have asked me to do some strange jobs. Once a doctor stopped me outside a hospital and asked me to take a skeleton to another hospital. And I did. But I asked the doctor to pay first – the skeleton couldn't pay, after all!

4 _____

Good question. I've always enjoyed being a taxi driver and I don't want to change. But of course, sometimes, it's not great. I don't like driving around without a passenger, but it's better than just waiting at the airport or at a railway station. I think that's the worst part – waiting.

2 **SPEAKING** **Look at the photos. Say how each picture is connected to the article.**

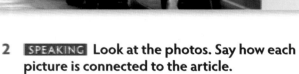
> There's a picture of a bus. She was a bus driver before she became a taxi driver.

3 **Read the interview again and answer the questions.**

1 Why did she stop being a bus driver?
2 Why was the famous actor angry when he got out of the taxi?
3 Why did she ask the doctor to pay first when she took the skeleton?
4 What two things does she not like about her job?

4 **SPEAKING** **Work in two groups. Group A: you are bus drivers. Group B: you are flight attendants. In your group, think of answers to these questions.**

1 When did you start your job?
2 Tell us about an accident you've had.
3 Tell us about a funny moment you've had.
4 Do you like your job or do you want to change?

5 **SPEAKING** **Work in pairs – one student from Group A with one student from Group B. Ask and answer the questions.**

6 **SPEAKING** **Decide whose answers were best: the bus driver's or the flight attendant's.**

GRAMMAR
Present perfect vs. past simple

1 Complete the things Fiona said in the article on page 114. Complete the rule with the names of the tenses.

1   I _____ film stars, politicians, you know, lots of famous people.
2   A year ago, a really famous actor _____ in my taxi.
3   People _____ all kinds of things.
4   One time, a passenger _____ a pair of false teeth.
5   People _____ me to do some strange jobs.
6   Once, a doctor _____ me outside a hospital and _____ me to take a skeleton to another hospital.

> **RULE:** Use the ¹_____ to talk about situations or actions at a particular time in the past.
>
> Use the ²_____ to talk about situations or actions in the past, when we don't say when they happened.

2 Find more examples of verbs in the past simple and present perfect in the article on page 114.

3 (Circle) the correct forms.

My name's Michael Edwards and I'm 26. ¹*I've been / I was* very lucky in my life because I have a good job and I travel a lot for work. ²*I've lived / I lived* in three different countries: Thailand, India and Singapore. ³*I've lived / I lived* in Singapore from 2012 to 2014. I live in Thailand now.

⁴*I've got / I got* married two years ago. My wife and I travel a lot together and ⁵*we've seen / we saw* some wonderful places. Last year ⁶*we've seen / we saw* the Taj Mahal in India.

⁷*I've done / I did* some crazy things in my life but the craziest was last month – ⁸*I've gone / I went* by minibus all the way to the north of Thailand. ⁹*It's been / It was* really scary!

> Workbook page 109 →

VOCABULARY
Transport and travel

1 ◀))2.43 Write the words under the photos. Listen and check.

~~a minibus~~ | a helicopter | a tram | a motorbike
a scooter | an underground train

0   *a minibus*

1   _____

2   _____

3   _____

4   _____

5   _____

Travel verbs

2 Complete the sentences with the correct form of the verbs in the list.

~~miss~~ | fly | catch | take | ride | drive

0   I had to walk home because I __*missed*__ the bus.
1   I ran very fast but I didn't _____ the train.
2   I have never _____ in a helicopter.
3   My brother's got a motorbike and now he's learning to _____ it.
4   We got in the car and we _____ to France.
5   The rain was terrible so we _____ a taxi.

3 SPEAKING Work in pairs. Ask each other questions. Use the verbs in Exercise 2 and the forms of transport you can see on this page and page 110.

> *Have you ever flown in a helicopter?*

> *No, I haven't. Have you ever taken a tram?*

> *Yes, I took a tram in Lisbon when I was on holiday.*

> Workbook page 110 →

Culture

1 **Look at the photos and answer the questions. Then say what you think the article is going to be about.**

Where can you see
- a student riding to school on a donkey?
- children walking to school along some rail tracks?

2 **◀))2.44 Read and listen to the article and say which country each photo is from.**

Hard journeys for schoolchildren

'How do you get to school?' This question often gets an answer like 'By bus' or 'I walk' or 'My parents take me by car'. But not always – there are children in many different parts of the world who, every day, have to go on a difficult journey in order to get to their lessons. They travel for kilometres on foot, or by boat, bicycle, donkey or train. They cross deserts, mountains, rivers, snow and ice: for example, the children of the Iñupiat community in Alaska go to school and then come back when it is dark, in extremely cold temperatures. And they are not the only ones – kids in many countries do this and more.

These children in Indonesia have to cross a bridge ten metres above a dangerous river to get to their class on time . (The bridge fell down in 2001 after very heavy rain.) Then they walk many more kilometres through the forest to their school in Banten village.

A pupil at Gulu Village Primary School, China, rides a donkey as his grandfather walks beside him. Gulu is a mountain village in a national park. The school is far away from the village. It is halfway up a mountain, so it takes five hours to climb from the bottom of the mountain to the school. The children have a dangerous journey: the path is only 45 centimetres wide in some places.

In Sri Lanka, some children have to cross a piece of wood between two walls of an old castle every morning. Their teacher watches them carefully. But in Sri Lanka, many girls don't go to school – they have to go to work or get married young. So girls are happy to take a risk in order to get to school.

Six-year old Fabricio Oliveira gets on his donkey every morning to ride with his friends for over an hour through a desert region in the very dry Sertão area of north-east Brazil. Their school is in Extrema. It's a tiny village – only very few people live there.

These children live in poor houses on Chetla Road in Delhi, India. Their homes are near the busy and dangerous railway lines that go to Alipur station. Every morning they walk along the tracks to get to their school, forty minutes away.

So one question we can ask is: why do the children do this? Because their parents make them do it? The answer, in many cases, is no – it's because for them going to school means a better future: They hope to get a job and money, so they can help their families and their neighbours . And this is why rivers, deserts or danger won't stop them on their way to school.

3 **Read the article again. What difficulties do children in these places face to get to school?**

1 The children of the Iñupiat community in Alaska.

2 The children who go to the school in Banten, Indonesia.

3 The children who go to the Gulu Village Primary School, China.

4 The children who go to school in Galle, Sri Lanka.

5 Fabricio Oliveira in Brazil.

6 The children who live along The Chetla Road in Delhi, India.

4 VOCABULARY **There are eight highlighted words in the article. Match the words with these meanings. Write the words.**

0	from one side to the other	*wide*
1	people living in houses near you	_____
2	a trip	_____
3	do something that can be dangerous	_____
4	a group of houses usually in the countryside	_____
5	the things that trains move on	_____
6	very, very small	_____
7	not late	_____

5 SPEAKING **Which journey is the one you would least like to have to do? Compare with others in the class.**

WRITING
Someone I admire

1 **Read Mariana's essay about 'Someone I admire'. Answer the questions.**

1 When and where was her uncle Tim born?

2 Where does he live now, and when did he move there?

3 How does he travel in his work?

4 What does he want to do in the future?

5 Why does Mariana admire her uncle?

2 **Find examples in the essay of the word *in* with these things.**

1 a year   3 a city

2 a month   4 a country

3 **Look at the four paragraphs of Mariana's essay about her uncle. Match the paragraphs with the contents.**

Paragraph 1	a	What he does, and how
Paragraph 2	b	Why she admires him
Paragraph 3	c	When and where he was born
Paragraph 4	d	Why he does these things

Someone I admire

(1) My uncle Tim is a really great guy. He was born in England in 1980, in a city called Halifax, but now he lives and works in Cambodia. He went to Cambodia in 2014.

(2) My uncle is a doctor and he worked at a hospital in Manchester for a few years. But in 2014 he decided to go and work in small villages in Cambodia because he heard that they needed doctors. He travels from village to village to help people. He has a small motorbike that he uses. Sometimes, though, he goes in a very small plane because the roads aren't good enough.

(3) Uncle Tim says that he wants to stay there because there is a lot of work to do. He has also met a girl there – he told me in an email that they are getting married in July next year. Uncle Tim hopes that he can help to teach Cambodian people to become doctors in the future. He has learned a lot of the language – that can't be easy!

(4) I said before that he's a great guy. Why do I think that? Well, because he is helping other people and is happy doing that, and because he has learned a lot about another culture.

4 **Think of someone that you admire: a famous person; or someone you know in your own life; or someone you invent.**

For the person, think about:

- facts about their life (when they were born, etc.)
- what they do, where and how, when they started
- what they want to do in the future
- why you admire them

5 **Write an essay called 'Someone I admire' in about 150 words. Use the example essay and language above to help you.**

READING AND WRITING

Part 5: Multiple-choice cloze ▸ Workbook page 53

1 Read the travel blog. Choose the best word (A, B or C) for each space.

I love **(0)** _travelling_ . I spend all my holidays visiting other countries. I never stay at home. So far I've **(1)**_____ to 56 different countries and this year, if I **(2)**_____ the money, I'll visit three more: Cambodia, Vietnam and Laos. It's a part of Asia I've **(3)**_____ been to so I'm really excited about this trip. I want to make the whole journey without **(4)**_____ a plane. I plan to get to Thailand by boat and then **(5)**_____ buses to visit these countries. On the way home, I'll travel **(6)**_____ train through China and India, and then through Europe. It **(7)**_____ be a short trip – it **(8)**_____ probably take about four months. I hope my boss doesn't mind me taking some time off work!

0	A travelling	B travel	C to travelling
1	A gone	B been	C went
2	A had	B will have	C have
3	A ever	B always	C never
4	A taking	B riding	C going
5	A travel	B miss	C take
6	A on	B by	C in
7	A isn't	B won't	C will
8	A will	B is	C can

(0 A travelling is circled)

Part 8: Information transfer ▸ Workbook page 107

2 Read the information about the school trip. Complete Gina's notes.

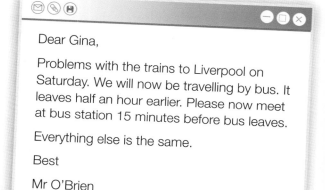

Dear Gina,

Problems with the trains to Liverpool on Saturday. We will now be travelling by bus. It leaves half an hour earlier. Please now meet at bus station 15 minutes before bus leaves.

Everything else is the same.

Best

Mr O'Brien

SCHOOL TRIP

Tate Art Museum Liverpool
Saturday 4th August

Train leaves at 10.15 am • Meet in station car park

£14 per person

School trip to the Tate Art Museum Liverpool

Date [1]_____

Travelling by [2]_____

Transport leaves at [3]_____

Meet at the [4]_____ about 9.30 am

Cost [5]£ [1]_____

LISTENING

Part 2: Matching ▸ Workbook page 61

3 🔊 **2.45** Listen to Jack talking to a friend about his transport project. How does each person get to school? For questions 1–5, write a letter (A–H) next to each person.

0	Jack	F
1	Olivia	
2	Rashid	
3	Morris	
4	Leslie	
5	Adam	

A bike
B boat
C taxi
D bus
E car
F on foot
G scooter
H train

TEST YOURSELF

VOCABULARY

1 Complete the sentences with the words in the list. There are two extra words.

neck | trams | ride | scooter | helicopter | tongue | caught | back | stomach ache | missed | lip | flew

1 He's really rich. He goes to work by _____ and he lands on the roof of his office building.
2 I've got a _____ . I think it was something I ate.
3 We _____ the last train home and so we slept in the station.
4 Open your mouth. I want to take a look at your _____ .
5 I can't _____ a motorbike and I don't want to learn how to. I think they're dangerous.
6 I fell and cut my mouth and made my top _____ bleed.
7 My dad rides his _____ to work. It's quicker than going by car and a lot cheaper.
8 We _____ over the mountains in a small plane. The views were fantastic!
9 I always sleep on my _____ .
10 Many cities are now using _____ to get people to and from work.

/10

GRAMMAR

2 Put the words in order to make sentences.

1 phone / I'll / home / you / get / soon / as / I / as
2 taxi / I / train, / miss / If / the / take / a / I'll
3 ever / Have / Europe / you / been / to / ?
4 seen / She's / sea / never / the
5 different / five / lived / countries / in / They've
6 grandchildren / be / easy / for / won't / our / Life

3 Find and correct the mistake in each sentence.

1 She's played football yesterday.
2 If we will be late, the teacher will be angry.
3 I have ever broken an arm or a leg.
4 I've never gone to America.
5 She has took a lot of photos on holiday.
6 One day in the future people will living on the moon.

/12

FUNCTIONAL LANGUAGE

4 Write the missing words.

1 A What's the _____ ?
   B My leg _____ a lot.
2 A I've _____ a headache.
   B I'm sorry to _____ that. Can I get you an aspirin?
3 A Have you _____ been to Canada?
   B No, I _____ .
4 A Do you think it _____ rain tomorrow?
   B I don't know. I'm not _____ .

/8

MY SCORE /30

| 22 – 30 |
| 10 – 21 |
| 0 – 9 |

PRONUNCIATION

UNIT 1
/s/, /z/, /ɪz/ sounds

1 🔊 **1.18** **Listen to the sentences.**

Gus makes cakes and sweets. He works hard and sleeps a lot.
James enjoys all kinds of games. He plays a lot of football with his friends.
Liz's job is fun. She washes and brushes horses and relaxes by riding them.

2 **Say the words with the /s/, /z/ and /ɪz/ endings.**

3 🔊 **1.19** **Listen and repeat. Then practise with a partner.**

UNIT 2
Contractions

1 🔊 **1.27** **Listen to the dialogue.**

TOM   Here's your pizza, Jane.
JANE That's not my pizza. I don't like cheese.
TOM   But Jane! They've all got cheese!
JANE No they haven't. There's one without it.
TOM   You're right ... it's this one. Here you are.

2 **Say the words in blue.**

3 🔊 **1.28** **Listen and repeat. Then practise with a partner.**

UNIT 3
Vowel sounds /ɪ/ and /iː/

1 🔊 **1.36** **Listen to the tongue twisters.**

Jill wishes she had fish and chips for dinner.
Pete's eating meat with cheese and peas.
Pete and Jill drink tea with milk.

2 **Say the words with the short /ɪ/ sound. Say the words with the long /iː/ sound.**

3 🔊 **1.37** **Listen and repeat. Then practise with a partner.**

UNIT 4
-er /ə/ at the end of words

1 🔊 **1.42** **Listen to the tongue twister.**

Jennifer's father's a firefighter,
Oliver's mother's a travel writer,
Peter's sister's a lorry driver;
And Amber's brother's a deep-sea diver.

2 **Say the words with the weak -er sound (the schwa /ə/).**

3 🔊 **1.43** **Listen and repeat. Then practise with a partner.**

UNIT 5
Regular past tense endings: /d/, /t/ and /ɪd/

1 🔊 **1.48** **Listen to the dialogue.**

MUM   What happened in the kitchen, Jack? It's a mess!
JACK I started to make a cake; then I decided to make a pizza. I cooked all morning and cleaned all afternoon.
MUM   You cleaned? What did you clean?
JACK My bedroom!

2 **Say the past tense words with the /d/, /t/ and /ɪd/ endings.**

3 🔊 **1.49** **Listen and repeat. Then practise with a partner.**

UNIT 6
Stressed syllables in words

1 🔊 **1.55** **Listen to the sentences.**

Sarah's funny, cheerful and helpful.
Jonathan's generous, confident and talented.
Elizabeth's intelligent, adventurous and easy-going.

2 **Say the two, three and four syllable words. Stress the words correctly.**

3 🔊 **1.56** **Listen and repeat. Then practise with a partner.**

UNIT 7
Vowel sounds: /ʊ/ and /uː/

1 🔊 **2.08** Listen to the dialogue.

LUKE   Let's look in this room, Sue.

SUE   Wow! It's got things from the moon in it.

LUKE   Look at these cool boots! I saw them in our science book.

SUE   We should take a photo for our school project, Luke.

2 Say the words with the short /ʊ/ vowel sound. Then say the words with the long /uː/ vowel sound.

3 🔊 **2.09** Listen and repeat. Then practise with a partner.

UNIT 8
Strong and weak forms of *was* and *were*

1 🔊 **2.13** Listen to the dialogue.

GIRL   Was she shopping?

BOY   Yes, she was. She was shopping for socks.

GIRL   Were they doing their homework?

BOY   No, they weren't. They were learning to surf!

2 Say the words with the /ɒ/ sound. Now say the words with the /ɜː/ sound. When *was* and *were* aren't stressed, we use the /ə/ sound. It's the same as /ɜː/ but shorter.

3 🔊 **2.14** Listen and repeat. Then practise with a partner.

UNIT 9
Vowel sounds: /ɪ/ and /aɪ/

1 🔊 **2.21** Listen to the dialogue.

JILL   I'd like to live in the wild. What about you, Mike?

MIKE   I prefer a city lifestyle. I don't like lions or tigers – or insects!

JILL   But living in the wild's much more exciting!

MIKE   Yes, Jill – and it's more frightening, too.

2 Say the words with the short /ɪ/ vowel sound. Then say the words with the long /aɪ/ vowel sound.

3 🔊 **2.22** Listen and repeat. Then practise with a partner.

UNIT 10
Voiced /ð/ and unvoiced /θ/ consonants

1 🔊 **2.27** Listen to the dialogue.

BETH   Look – there's the theatre.

HARRY That's not the right one, Beth.

BETH   Well, it says, 'The Fifth Avenue Theatre'.

HARRY But we want the one on Third Street!

2 Say the words with the voiced /ð/. Then say the words with the unvoiced /θ/.

3 🔊 **2.28** Listen and repeat. Then practise with a partner.

UNIT 11
The /h/ consonant sound

1 🔊 **2.32** Listen to the dialogue.

DR HARRIS   Who's next? Oh, hello Harry. How can I help you?

HARRY   Well, Dr Harris – my head's very hot!

DR HARRIS   Let me see ... does it hurt here?

HARRY   Yes, doctor! That feels horrible!

DR HARRIS   It's your hat, Harry. It's too small!

2 Say the words starting with the /h/ consonant sound.

3 🔊 **2.33** Listen and repeat. Then practise with a partner.

UNIT 12
Sentence stress

1 🔊 **2.41** Listen to the stress in these sentences.

<u>Car</u> – <u>plane</u> – <u>bike</u> – <u>train</u>.
A <u>car</u>, a <u>plane</u>, a <u>bike</u>, a <u>train</u>.
A <u>car</u> and a <u>plane</u> and a <u>bike</u> and a <u>train</u>.
A <u>car</u> and then a <u>plane</u> and then a <u>bike</u> and then a <u>train</u>.

2 Which words are stressed in every sentence? What happens to the other words?

3 🔊 **2.42** Listen and repeat. Then practise with a partner.

UNIT 1
Adverbs of frequency

> Words like *sometimes*, *never*, *always* come <u>between</u> the subject and the verb or adjective.
>
> ✓ I **sometimes do** my homework on Saturday.
> ✗ I ~~do sometimes~~ my homework on Saturday.

Correct the six adverbs that are in the wrong place.

I have always fun on Saturday! In the morning, I usually meet my friends in the park or they come sometimes to my house. In the afternoon, we go often swimming. I never do homework on Saturday. In the evening, we have always pizza. My mum usually cooks the pizza at home, but we go occasionally to a restaurant. I always am very tired on Sunday!

like + -*ing*

> We use the -*ing* form of the verb after verbs expressing likes and dislikes.
>
> ✓ He **likes watching** TV.   ✗ He ~~likes watch~~ TV.

Find five mistakes in the conversation. Correct them.

LUCY   What do you like doing, Jim?

JIM   I love play with my dog, Spud.

LUCY   Does he enjoy swim?

JIM   No, he hates swim. But he likes go to the beach.

LUCY   I like play on the beach, too!

UNIT 2
Verbs of perception

> We use the present simple with verbs of perception (*look, taste, sound, smell*) to talk about something that is true now. We don't use the present continuous.
>
> ✓ His new jacket **looks** terrible!
> ✗ His new jacket ~~is looking terrible~~!

> We use *look, taste, sound, smell* + adjective, NOT *look, taste, sound, smell* + *like* + adjective.
>
> ✓ This pizza **tastes awful**!
> ✗ This pizza ~~tastes like awful~~!

<u>Underline</u> **the correct sentence.**

1   a   I think this jacket looks expensive.
    b   I think this jacket is looking expensive.
2   a   Your weekend sounds great!
    b   Your weekend sounds like great!
3   a   Look at that dog. He looks like happy.
    b   Look at that dog. He looks happy.
4   a   The music is sounding beautiful.
    b   The music sounds beautiful.

Present continuous

> We form the present continuous with the present simple of *be* before the -*ing* form (e.g. *running, doing, wearing*, etc.) of the main verb, i.e. subject + *be* + -*ing* form of the verb.
>
> ✓ I **am looking** at the sky.
> ✗ ~~I looking~~ at the sky.

> But in questions, we use the present simple of *be* <u>before</u> the person doing the action, i.e. *be* + subject + -*ing* form of verb.
>
> ✓ **Why are you looking** at the sky?
> ✗ ~~Why you are looking~~ at the sky?

Put the correct form of *be* in the correct place in the sentences.

1   What you looking at?
2   They going shopping today.
3   I looking for a new jacket.
4   She wearing a beautiful dress.
5   Why he laughing? It's not funny!

UNIT 3
much and *many*

> We use *many* with plural countable nouns and *much* with uncountable nouns.
>
> ✓ How **many** sandwiches have you got?
> ✗ How ~~much~~ sandwiches have you got?
> ✓ We haven't got **much** cheesecake.
> ✗ We haven't got ~~many~~ cheesecake.

Read the conversation. (Circle) much or many.

SARAH Hi, Julian, have we got everything we need for the party?

JULIAN We've got some crisps, but we haven't got [1]*many / much* fruit.

SARAH How [2]*many / much* apples did you buy?

JULIAN We've got six apples, but we haven't got [3]*many / much* vegetables.

SARAH I've got four tomatoes. How [4]*many / much* people are coming?

JULIAN Everybody from our class is coming!

SARAH Oh, have we got [5]*many / much* juice?

JULIAN Yes, but we haven't got [6]*many / much* glasses.

SARAH Oh dear! We've got a problem.

too + adjective and (*not*) + adjective + *enough*

> We use *too* + adjective to say there is more than is necessary of something. We never use *too much* + adjective.
>
> ✓ The soup was **too cold**.
> ✗ The soup was ~~too much cold~~.
>
> We use *not* before the adjective and *enough* <u>after</u> the adjective to say there is less than is necessary of something.
>
> ✓ The soup was**n't hot enough**.
> ✗ The soup ~~wasn't enough hot~~.

Write a cross (✗) next to the incorrect sentences. Then write the correct sentences.

1 We didn't go because the weather wasn't enough good. ☐

2 The sausages were too spicy. And the pizza wasn't warm enough. ☐

3 I didn't do my homework. I was too much tired. ☐

4 The food he eats is healthy not enough. ☐

5 The room wasn't enough big and the price was too much expensive. ☐

UNIT 4
Possessive adjectives and pronouns

> We don't use *a/an* or *the* before possessive adjectives or possessive pronouns.
>
> ✓ This is **my sister**.
> ✗ This is ~~the my sister~~.
> ✓ This is **mine**. Where is **yours**?
> ✗ This is ~~the mine~~. Where is ~~the yours~~?

Find five mistakes in the conversation. Correct them.

CLARA Hi Ben, is that your phone?

BEN No, it's a my brother's. His is black and the mine's blue. The one on the table is the mine.

CLARA Oh, it's great! I need a new phone. The mine is really old!

BEN When is your birthday? Maybe your mum will give you a new phone.

CLARA Hmm. But the my birthday is in December! I need a new phone now!

Possessive *'s*

> We don't usually use noun + *of* + noun to talk about possession. We use name or noun + *'s*.
>
> ✓ That is **my cousin's house**.
> ✗ That is ~~the house of my cousin~~.

Rewrite these sentences using *'s*.

1 She's the sister of my best friend.

2 They are the grandparents of my cousin.

3 Is that the brother of your best friend?

4 She's the sister of my mum.

5 That's the phone of my brother.

you, *your* or *yours*?

> We use *you* to refer to the subject or object. We use *your* to talk about possession.
>
> ✓ Thank you very much for **your letter**.
> ✗ Thank you very much for ~~you letter~~.
>
> We use *your* before a noun for possession. We use *yours* to replace *your* + noun.
>
> ✓ Is this **your phone**? ✓ Is this **phone yours**?
> ✗ Is this ~~yours phone~~?

Circle the correct word to complete the letter.

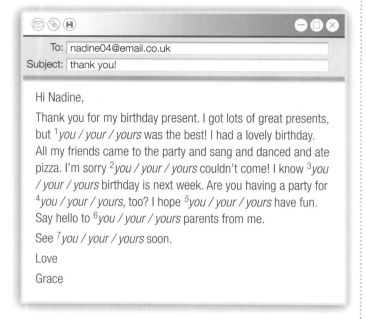

To: nadine04@email.co.uk
Subject: thank you!

Hi Nadine,

Thank you for my birthday present. I got lots of great presents, but ¹*you / your / yours* was the best! I had a lovely birthday. All my friends came to the party and sang and danced and ate pizza. I'm sorry ²*you / your / yours* couldn't come! I know ³*you / your / yours* birthday is next week. Are you having a party for ⁴*you / your / yours*, too? I hope ⁵*you / your / yours* have fun. Say hello to ⁶*you / your / yours* parents from me.

See ⁷*you / your / yours* soon.

Love

Grace

UNIT 5
Modifiers: *quite, very, really*

Remember: we use modifier + adjective (+ noun). We don't use noun + modifier + adjective.

✓ Pompeii has **a lot of very old buildings**.
✗ Pompeii has a lot of ~~buildings very old~~.
✓ The buildings are **very old**.

Be careful when you write these words.

- We write *quite* with the e **after** the *t*. Don't confuse *quite* with the adjective *quiet*.
  ✓ This chair is **quite** comfortable.
  ✗ This chair is ~~quiet~~ comfortable.
- We write *really* with two *l*s.
  ✓ Pompeii is **really** interesting.
  ✗ Pompeii is ~~realy~~ interesting.
- We write *very* with one *r*.
  ✓ Their house is **very** big.
  ✗ Their house is ~~verry~~ big.

Find seven mistakes. Correct them.

We went to see our new house on Sunday. My dad wants to live near his office. It's realy annoying for me because a lot of my friends live near my house now. I was very sad when we went into the house. But when I saw inside it, I was amazed really! It looked quiet small, but inside it was really big. It had a kitchen really big and the bedrooms were verry big too. But the best thing was the garden. It was beautiful really, with a swimming pool very big and lots of trees. I think my friends will like visiting my new house!

UNIT 6
Past simple (regular and irregular verbs)

To make any verb negative in the past simple we use *didn't* + the base form of the verb. We don't use *didn't* + past simple. Remember to use the base form of regular and irregular verbs.

✓ We **didn't visit** the LEGO house.
✗ We ~~didn't visited~~ the LEGO house.

Circle the correct answer.

1 I'm sorry I didn't *come / came* to your party.
2 We didn't *went / go* on holiday last year.
3 I looked everywhere, but I didn't *found / find* my phone.
4 We visited the art gallery but we didn't *see / saw* anything interesting.
5 We didn't *spend / spent* a lot of time in Paris. It was too hot!
6 I didn't *knew / know* you liked One Direction.

Double genitive

We form the double genitive with noun + *of* + possessive pronoun (*mine, yours, his, hers, ours, yours, theirs*). We don't use object pronouns (*me, you, him, her, our, your, their*) to form the double genitive.

✓ She's a **friend of mine**.
✗ She's a friend ~~of me~~.

We also form the double genitive with noun + *of* + possessive adjective (*my, your, his, her, our, your, their*) + noun + possessive *'s*.

✓ She's a **friend of my sister's**.
✗ She's a friend ~~of my sister~~.

Circle the correct answer.

1 Lisa is a good friend of *me / my / mine*.
2 Matt Damon is a favourite actor of my *sister / sister's*.
3 My brother went to the cinema with a friend of *him / he's / his*.
4 I met a cousin of *Rory's / Rory* at the party.
5 She brought a new classmate of *hers / her / she's* to the party.
6 Isn't that woman a teacher of *your / you / yours*?

UNIT 7
have to / don't have to

> We always use the base form of the verb after *have to / don't have to*.
>
> ✓ He **has to tidy** his room today.
> ✗ He has to ~~tidied~~ his room today.
> ✗ He has to ~~tidying~~ his room today.
>
> We use the correct form of *do + not/n't + have to* to say that something isn't necessary. We don't use *haven't to*.
>
> ✓ You **don't have to help** me. I can do it.
> ✗ You ~~haven't to~~ help me. I can do it.

Find six mistakes. Correct them.

I have to do a lot of housework at home, but I'm OK about that. I have to tidying my room, but I haven't to vacuum the floor. My brother has to does that. We have to do the washing up, but we don't have do the washing. My dad does that once a week. I haven't to do the cooking – my mum likes cooking. She says it helps her to relax. Of course, I have to doing my homework every day after school. I'm not OK about that!

UNIT 8
Past continuous vs. past simple

> We use the past continuous to talk about background actions in the past, and the past simple for actions which happened at one moment in the past.
>
> ✓ I **was watching** television when the lights **went** out.
> ✗ I ~~watched~~ television when the lights went out.

Complete the story with the past continuous or past simple of the verb in brackets.

The surprise!

It [1]_____ (happen) last Saturday while I [2]_____ (have) a party at my house. At 9 o'clock, we [3]_____ (dance) and having a fantastic time. Then, suddenly, the lights [4]_____ (go) out. I [5]_____ (close) my eyes and screamed! But when I [6]_____ (stop), I heard that all my friends [7]_____ (laugh). When I [8]_____ (open) my eyes, everybody was smiling at me. When my mum [9]_____ (arrive) with a cake and candles, I finally understood …

UNIT 9
Comparative adjectives

> We use *more* + adjective with two syllables or more to form the comparative. We don't use *more* with adjectives with one syllable or with adjectives that are already in the comparative form (e.g. *smaller, colder, friendlier*).
>
> ✓ His room is **smaller** than mine.
> ✗ His room is ~~more small~~ than mine.
> ✗ His room is ~~more smaller~~ than mine.

Underline the correct sentence.

1. a Lions can run more faster during the night.
   b Lions can run faster during the night.
2. a The weather in the Kalahari is drier than in Europe.
   b The weather in the Kalahari is more dry than in Europe.
3. a It's more hotter in the summer than in the winter.
   b It's hotter in the summer than in the winter.
4. a People in the countryside are friendlier than people in the city.
   b People in the countryside are more friendlier than people in the city.

can / can't for ability

> We always use the base form of the verb after *can / can't*.
>
> ✓ He **can swim**, but he **can't surf**.
> ✗ He can ~~swam~~, but he can't ~~to surf~~.

Circle the correct verb form.

1. I love living by the sea. On sunny days, I can *went / going / go* to the beach.
2. On cold days, you can *do / doing / to do* the shopping in the town centre.
3. We can *learning / learn / to learn* a lot about wildlife from nature programmes.
4. You can't *drive / driving / drove* a car if you're fifteen.
5. They can't **to** *come / coming / come* to the party because they're on holiday.

UNIT 10
be going to for intentions

We use the present tense of *be* + *going to* + base form of the verb to talk about our intentions in the future. Remember to use the present tense of *be*.

✓ He **is going to study** all weekend.
✗ He ~~going~~ to study all weekend.

Complete the sentences with *be going to* and the verb in brackets.

1 He _____ (paint) his bedroom on Saturday.
2 I've bought a new chair. I _____ (put) it near the TV.
3 We _____ (visit) my cousin because he is ill.
4 They _____ (go) to the sports centre by car.
5 We _____ (watch) a film tonight.

Present continuous for arrangements

We use the present continuous to talk about arrangements for the future. We don't use the present simple.

✓ **I'm going to visit** my grandparents tomorrow.
✗ I ~~go~~ to visit my grandparents tomorrow.

To ask questions about arrangements, we use question word + *be* + subject + the *-ing* form of the verb. Remember to put the words in the correct order.

✓ What **are you doing** tomorrow?
✗ What ~~you are doing~~ tomorrow?

Find six mistakes in the dialogue. Correct them.

LARA   Hi Sam, what you are doing on Saturday?

SAM   Well, in the morning, I play football in the park.

LARA   What are you doing in the afternoon?

SAM   I don't do anything. What are you doing?

LARA   I paint my bedroom.

SAM   Cool! What colour do you use?

LARA   I'm going to choose the colour when I go to the shop.

SAM   Which shop are you going to?

LARA   I go to the shop in the high street at 2 o'clock.

SAM   OK. I'll meet you there! I can help you to choose.

UNIT 11
will / won't for future predictions

We use the present continuous to talk about things happening now and future arrangements. We use *will* or *won't* + base form to make future predictions.

✓ I'm sure you**'ll do** well in your test next week.
✗ I'm sure you ~~are doing~~ well in your test next week.
✓ **I'm going** to a party on Saturday.
✗ I ~~will go~~ to a party on Saturday.

Choose present continuous or *'ll / won't* to complete the email.

Hi Gareth,

I don't think [1] *I'll see / I'm seeing* you before my holiday. [2] *We'll leave / We're leaving* on Saturday, so [3] *I'm being / I'll be* very busy. [4] *I'll go / I'm going* shopping on Friday, so [5] *I'm not being / I won't be* at art class. [6] *I'll need / I'm needing* to buy some shorts – my dad says [7] *it'll be / it's being* really hot in Tunisia! [8] *I'll phone / I'm phoning* you on Friday night if I have time. I have to go now. [9] *I'll help / I'm helping* my sister with her homework.

Marcus

UNIT 12
Present perfect simple

We use the present perfect simple to talk about situations or actions that happened some time in the past.

✓ I **have met** a lot of famous actors.
✗ I ~~met~~ a lot of famous actors.

We use the past simple to talk about situations or actions at a specific time in the past.

✓ A year ago, I **met** a famous actor.
✗ A year ago, I ~~have met~~ a famous actor.

Find seven mistakes in the text. Correct them.

My parents work for international companies, so I travelled a lot. I've lived in Europe, Asia and the USA. Two years ago, I have lived in Spain for six months. My brother's only three, so he only went to Europe and he forgot that trip! My dad travelled to more places. He has been to Australia and New Zealand last year, but we never visited England.

STUDENT A

UNIT 2, PAGE 23

Student A

1   You are a customer in a sports shop. You like a pair of trainers.

You want a black pair.

You want to know the price.

You want to try them on.

2   You are an assistant in a clothes shop. Student B likes a sweatshirt. It's €36.95. You have green, blue or red.

UNIT 5, PAGE 55

Student A

You and your friend have got £200. You are at a flea market buying furniture for a new room for your youth club. These are the prices of the pieces of furniture:

- 2 armchairs £30
- cooker £20
- shelf £5
- table with 8 chairs £70
- desk and lamp £25
- sofa £75
- large carpet £70
- mirror £10
- wardrobe £30
- small carpet £30
- sofa £40
- 8 posters of film stars £5

You want to buy the 2 armchairs, the large carpet, the cooker and the posters.

You do not want to buy the shelf or the wardrobe.

You are uncertain about the table with the 8 chairs and the sofas.

Have a conversation and agree on what to buy.

UNIT 7, PAGE 73

Student A

You are a son or daughter. You are at home.

You want to see a friend.

You are phoning your mum or dad about it.

When your mum/dad tells you that you should do some housework, ask her/him what you have to do.

Also, tell your mum/dad that there are some things she/he shouldn't forget. When she/he asks you what things, say:

She/He …

- should do the shopping
- shouldn't be late tonight (you want to watch a DVD together with her/him)
- mustn't forget to bring some chocolate biscuits!

The line is not very good so you have to ask your mum or dad several times to repeat what she/he has said.

UNIT 11, PAGE 107

Student A

Ask your questions and answer Student B's.

1   What will you do if it rains this weekend?
2   What will you do if the weather's nice?
3   How will you feel if your teacher gives you a lot of homework today?
4   What will you wear if you go out to a party this evening?
5   What film will you see if you go to the cinema this week?
6   What programme will you watch if you watch TV this evening?

STUDENT B

UNIT 2, PAGE 23

Student B

1 You are an assistant in a sports shop.
Student A likes a pair of trainers. They're €34.99.
You only have brown or red (not black).

2 You are a customer in a clothes shop. You like a sweatshirt.
You want a green one.
You want to know the price.
You want to try it on.

UNIT 5, PAGE 55

Student B

You and your friend have got £200. You are at a flea market buying furniture for a new room for your youth club. These are the prices of the pieces of furniture:

- 2 armchairs £30
- cooker £20
- shelf £5
- table with 8 chairs £70
- desk and lamp £25
- sofa £75
- large carpet £70
- mirror £10
- wardrobe £30
- small carpet £30
- sofa £40
- 8 posters of film stars £5

You want to buy the table with the 8 chairs, the cooker, the large carpet, and one of the sofas.

You do not want to buy the 2 armchairs or the posters.

You are uncertain about the desk and the lamp.

Have a conversation and agree on what to buy.

UNIT 7, PAGE 73

Student B

You are a mum or dad. Your son/daughter is phoning you.

Make sure he/she knows that he/she has to do some housework before he/she can go out. When he/she asks you, say:

He/She …

- has to tidy up his/her room
- should load the dishwasher
- mustn't forget to vacuum the floor

When your son or daughter tells you that there are things you shouldn't forget, ask them what things.

The line is not very good so you have to ask your son or daughter several times to repeat what he/she has said.

UNIT 11, PAGE 107

Student B

Ask your questions and answer Student A's.

1 What will you do if you stay at home this weekend?

2 What will you study if you go to university?

3 What will you buy if you go shopping this weekend?

4 How will you feel if your parents ask you to do a lot of housework this evening?

5 What video game will you play if you decide to play video games this evening?

6 Where will you go if you meet your friends tonight?